WORLD
HISTORY SERIES

Westward Expansion

by
Michael V. Uschan

Lucent Books, P.O. Box 289011, San Diego, CA 92198-9011

For Lisa, Julie, and Joel (J. J.) Meincke: I hope your journeys through life will be as fullfilling as the treks pioneers made across America to create a nation stretching from "sea to shining sea."

Library of Congress Cataloging-in-Publication Data

Uschan, Michael V., 1948–
    Westward Expansion / by Michael Uschan.
        p.   cm.— (World history series)
    Includes bibliographical references and index.
    Summary: Describes the history of American westward expansion, including the exploration of the frontier to the Pacific Ocean, the establishment of the Lone Star State and the Mormon kingdom of Deseret, Manifest Destiny, the California gold rush, the population of the plains, and the legacy of the American frontier.
    ISBN 1-56006-690-3 (hardcover : alk. paper)
    1. United States—Territorial expansion—Juvenile literature. 2. Frontier and pioneer life—United States—Juvenile literature. 3. Frontier and pioneer life—West (U.S.)—Juvenile literature. 4. West (U.S.)—Discovery and exploration—Juvenile literature. 5. Overland journeys to the Pacific—Juvenile literature. [1. United States—Territorial expansion. 2. West (U.S.)—Discovery and Exploration. 3. Frontier and pioneer life—West (U.S.)] I. Title. II. Series.
E179.5.U83 2001
978'.02—dc21   00-008639
                                                                   CIP
                                                                    AC

Copyright 2001 by Lucent Books, Inc., P.O. Box 289011, San Diego, California 92198-9011

Printed in the U.S.A.

Contents

Foreword

Each year on the first day of school, nearly every history teacher faces the task of explaining why his or her students should study history. One logical answer to this question is that exploring what happened in our past explains how the things we often take for granted—our customs, ideas, and institutions—came to be. As statesman and historian Winston Churchill put it, "Every nation or group of nations has its own tale to tell. Knowledge of the trials and struggles is necessary to all who would comprehend the problems, perils, challenges, and opportunities which confront us today." Thus, a study of history puts modern ideas and institutions in perspective. For example, though the founders of the United States were talented and creative thinkers, they clearly did not invent the concept of democracy. Instead, they adapted some democratic ideas that had originated in ancient Greece and with which the Romans, the British, and others had experimented. An exploration of these cultures, then, reveals their very real connection to us through institutions that continue to shape our daily lives.

Another reason often given for studying history is the idea that lessons exist in the past from which contemporary societies can benefit and learn. This idea, although controversial, has always been an intriguing one for historians. Those who agree that society can benefit from the past often quote philosopher George Santayana's famous statement, "Those who cannot remember the past are condemned to repeat it." Historians who subscribe to Santayana's philosophy believe that, for example, studying the events that led up to the major world wars or other significant historical events would allow society to chart a different and more favorable course in the future.

Just as difficult as convincing students to realize the importance of studying history is the search for useful and interesting supplementary materials that present historical events in a context that can be easily understood. The volumes in Lucent Books' World History Series attempt to present a broad, balanced, and penetrating view of the march of history. Ancient Egypt's important wars and rulers, for example, are presented against the rich and colorful backdrop of Egyptian religious, social, and cultural developments. The series engages the reader by enhancing historical events with these cultural contexts. For example, in Ancient Greece, the text covers the role of women in that society. Slavery is discussed in The Roman Empire, as well as how slaves earned their freedom. The numerous and varied aspects of everyday life in these and other societies are explored in each volume of the series. Additionally, the series covers the major political, cultural, and philosophical ideas as the torch of civilization is passed from ancient Mesopotamia and Egypt, through Greece, Rome, Medieval Europe, and other world cultures, to the modern day.

The material in the series is formatted in a thorough, precise, and organized manner. Each volume offers the reader a comprehensive and clearly written overview of an important historical event or period. The topic under discussion is placed in a broad, historical context. For example, The Italian Renaissance begins with a discussion of the High Middle Ages and the loss of central control that allowed certain Italian cities to develop artistically. The book ends by looking forward to the Reformation and interpreting the societal changes that grew out of the Renaissance. Thus, students are not only involved in an historical era, but also enveloped by the events leading up to that era and the events following it.

One important and unique feature in the World History Series is the primary and secondary source quotations that richly supplement each volume. These quotes are useful in a number of ways. First, they allow students access to sources they would not normally be exposed to because of the difficulty and obscurity of the original source. The quotations range from interesting anecdotes to farsighted cultural perspectives and are drawn from historical witnesses both past and present. Second, the quotes demonstrate how and where historians themselves derive their information on the past as they strive to reach a consensus on historical events. Lastly, all of the quotes are footnoted, familiarizing students with the citation process and allowing them to verify quotes and/or look up the original source if the quote piques their interest.

Finally, the books in the World History Series provide a detailed launching point for further research. Each book contains a bibliography specifically geared toward student research. A second, annotated bibliography introduces students to all the sources the author consulted when compiling the book. A chronology of important dates gives students an overview, at a glance, of the topic covered. Where applicable, a glossary of terms is included.

In short, the series is designed not only to acquaint readers with the basics of history, but also to make them aware that their lives are a part of an ongoing human saga. Perhaps they will then come to the same realization as famed historian Arnold Toynbee. In his monumental work, *A Study of History*, he wrote about becoming aware of history flowing through him in a mighty current, and of his own life "welling like a wave in the flow of this vast tide."

Important Dates in the History of Westward Expansion

1783
(September 3) The Treaty of Paris signed to end the Revolutionary War and give the United States of America its freedom from Great Britain.

1804
(May 14) Meriwether Lewis and William Clark begin their exploration of the Louisiana Territory.

1834
(June 30) The Indian Territory established in what is now Oklahoma as a new home for Native Americans displaced by white settlers.

1783	1805	1810	1826	1831	1836

1803
(April 30) United States purchases the Louisiana Territory from France for $15 million.

1806
(Sept. 23) Lewis and Clark return from exploring the Louisiana Territory.

1810
(Oct. 27) United States annexes West Florida, a Spanish possession composed of territory that today includes parts of Alabama, Louisiana, and Mississippi.

1836
(Feb. 23–March 6) A Mexican army led by General Santa Anna attacks the Alamo and after a long siege defeats and kills the defenders. (April 21) A force led by Sam Houston defeats Santa Anna's army to win independence for Texas from Mexico.

1819
(Feb. 22) United States annexes East Florida, which makes up the present day state of Florida.

1844
(April 12) United States signs a treaty with the Republic of Texas to annex an area that includes Texas and parts of what are now Colorado, New Mexico, and Oklahoma.

1846
(Feb. 10) The Mormons begin leaving Nauvoo, Illinois, to head west to their new home in what will become Utah. (May 8) Mexican War begins with the Battle of Palo Alto.

1848
(Jan. 24) James Marshall discovers gold in California while building a sawmill on the American River for Johann A. Sutter. (Feb. 2) Mexico and the United States sign the Treaty of Guadalupe-Hidalgo, ending the Mexican-American War; the United States gains what is now California, Nevada, Utah, and parts of Colorado, New Mexico, Arizona, and Wyoming. (Aug. 14) United States annexes the Oregon Territory containing what is now Idaho, Oregon, Washington, and parts of Montana and Wyoming.

1853
(Dec. 30) Gadsden Purchase approved. For $10 million, the United States buys 29,640 square-miles of territory from Mexico that today is part of Arizona and New Mexico.

1841	1850	1860	1870	1890	1895

1867
(March 30) United States purchases the Alaska Territory from Russia for $7.2 million.

1869
(May 10) The rails of the Union Pacific and Central Pacific railroads joined in a ceremony at Promontory Point near Ogden, Utah; (October) trains begin to roll cross-country.

1893
(Jan. 7) Queen Liliuokalani arrested in a coup led by American businessmen, bringing Hawaii under U.S. control.

1889
(April 22–23) A huge portion of Indian Territory is opened for white settlement in the Oklahoma Land Rush.

1847
(Sept. 14) American forces take Mexico City in a decisive battle that wins the war and ends the fighting.

1845
(March 1) President John Tyler signs the joint resolution of Congress to annex Texas. (July) John L. O'Sullivan coins the term Manifest Destiny in the July-August issue of *The United States Magazine and Democratic Review*.

History's "Greatest Migration"

When Thomas Jefferson was a young boy, he and his father would climb to the top of a small mountain for an exhilarating view of Shadwell, the family plantation in Virginia. As the future president and author of the Declaration of Independence gazed at the towering Blue Ridge Mountains, his eager, questioning mind would soar over them into the mysterious frontier that lay even further west.

> "What lies beyond the mountains?" he asked his father.
>
> "More mountains."
>
> "And beyond them?"
>
> "A big river—the Mississippi."
>
> "And beyond the river?"
>
> Peter Jefferson shrugged. "Nobody knows for sure." [1]

When Jefferson was born in 1743, Shadwell was just one hundred miles east of the frontier, that vast, unknown land, that both stirred the imaginations of colonists and frightened them with its danger. Three decades later when Jefferson penned the Declaration of Independence and then helped the thirteen colonies win their freedom from Great Britain, the United States was still only a narrow strip of land several hundred miles wide hugging the Atlantic Ocean.

Yet within a century, the relentless yearning of Americans for more land, more wealth, and more adventure would push the nation's borders three thousand miles west to the Pacific Ocean in what historian Frederick Merk calls history's most epic mass migration:

> The Westward Movement across the continent was not merely prolonged, but massive. It brought uncounted millions from the Old World to the New, and from the shores of the Atlantic to the Pacific. It was the greatest migration of peoples in recorded history. It was magnificent in its achievements. It replaced barbarism with civilization. It unlocked the bounties of nature and made them a blessing to mankind. It bent reluctant and unfriendly forces of nature to man's will and control. It created a nation. [2]

But in *History of the Westward Movement*, Merk also admits "some aspects of the [Westward] Movement were less attractive. Conquest, speculation, exploitation, and violence were all part of this crusade into the wilderness. They were the harsher realities of the movement, and the source of some of the nation's [ongoing] problems." [3]

And in *The Story of America*, editor Carroll C. Calkins writes that the tragedy associated with this great achievement was the destruction of a way of life for millions of Native Americans:

> For [them], the American dream has been nothing less than a nightmare. From the landing of the first English settlers at the beginning of the 17th century to the closing of the last frontier, the Indians have been the victims of almost unrelieved woe. Those tribes that escaped annihilation by the white man's bullets and disease suffered instead something close to cultural genocide. Wherever the white man moved west he displaced the Indian by force of arms, by destroying his hunting grounds, or by fraudulent treaties in which the uncomprehending red man often exchanged his patrimony for glittering trinkets. [4]

THE AMERICAN DREAM

The American Dream that lured English settlers to Jamestown, Virginia, in 1607, the Pilgrims to Plymouth, Massachusetts, thirteen years later, and tens of millions of

Children rejoice as two hunters bring home enough meat for many nourishing meals. Pioneers had to grow or hunt all the food they ate.

new Americans to this country since then has never changed. It has always been the promise of freedom, wealth, and a better way of life. Historian Marshall B. Davidson claims that even the earliest colonists who ventured to the New World had a burning desire to explore unknown territory beyond their borders:

> When the people of Newtown, Massachusetts, wanted to move Westward into Connecticut in the seventeenth century they gave as one of their reasons "the strong bent of their spirits to remove thither." Nothing else more concisely explains the steady westward migration of Americans. Greener pastures, blacker soil, more golden hills, gave express purpose to those who longed for one. But the "bent" was ingrained. If hell lay to the West, ran a proverb, Americans would cross heaven to reach it. [5]

This restless, relentless yearning to see what was over the next hill or around the next bend of the river and to tap its riches was a fever that would infect Americans over and over again, luring them ever westward. In the early eighteenth century, mountain men journeyed to the Rocky Mountains to trap beaver, blazing trails across the continent that would be traveled in succeeding decades by millions of farmers, miners, ranchers, and others pursuing their individual dreams.

As the numbers of Americans grew, so did their need for land. The U.S. population in 1790 was only 3.9 million, a figure that by 1810 had nearly doubled to 7.2 million and by 1850 had increased nearly eight times to 23.1 million; thereafter the population would double again every twenty-five years for the rest of the century. This population explosion was fueled by natural increase and a tidal wave of immigrants: 151,824 newcomers in the decade ending in 1830, more than 599,000 in the next ten years, 1.7 million more by 1850, and another 2.6 million by 1860, the high point of U.S. immigration until 1890, when 5.2 million arrived in one year.

THE GOVERNMENT BACKS EXPANSION

As early as 1817 this explosive growth led future vice president John C. Calhoun to comment, "We are greatly, and rapidly—I was about to say fearfully—growing!" [6]

The South Carolina congressman, however, was one of the leaders who supported Americans as they kept extending the nation's boundary ever westward. In 1803 President Jefferson engineered the Louisiana Purchase, doubling the nation's size to 1.8 million square miles and pushing its borders west to the Rocky Mountains. By 1840 the government was backing migration all the way to the Pacific Ocean.

When settlers began moving into Oregon Country—an area that included present-day Oregon, Idaho, Washington, and parts of Montana and Wyoming—Missouri Senator Thomas Hart Benton pledged U.S. support even though England still claimed joint ownership. "The American population," Benton proclaimed, "has begun to extend itself to the Oregon Country. I say to

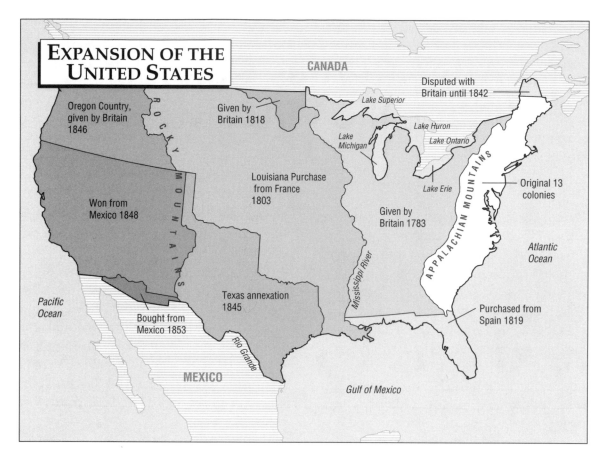

EXPANSION OF THE UNITED STATES

CANADA

Oregon Country, given by Britain 1846

Given by Britain 1818

Disputed with Britain until 1842

Lake Superior

Lake Huron

Lake Michigan

Lake Ontario

ROCKY MOUNTAINS

Louisiana Purchase from France 1803

Lake Erie

APPALACHIAN MOUNTAINS

Original 13 colonies

Won from Mexico 1848

Given by Britain 1783

Atlantic Ocean

Pacific Ocean

Bought from Mexico 1853

Texas annexation 1845

Mississippi River

Purchased from Spain 1819

Rio Grande

MEXICO

Gulf of Mexico

---

them all, 'Go on! the Government will follow you, and will give you protection and land!'" [7]

Benton and others rallied around the cry of Manifest Destiny, the belief that Americans were chosen by God to rule the continent. Manifest Destiny was based in part on racist theories that convinced its followers it was not only their right but their duty to subjugate Native Americans, Mexicans, Hawaiians, and other groups so they could teach them the benefits of white, Christian civilization. Manifest Destiny thus justified the injustices done to these groups while the nation was being created.

THE WEST IS QUICKLY SETTLED

As an adult, Jefferson was still intrigued with the wilderness. When the Louisiana Purchase extended America's borders, Jefferson predicted the transaction would provide enough land for the unlimited settlement of "our descendants to the hundredth and thousandth generation." [8]

But Jefferson grossly underestimated the speed of that process. Within only four generations an onrushing tide of hardy, adventurous pioneers would push the nation's boundaries all the way to the Pacific Ocean.

1 Adventurous Colonists Brave the Wilderness

Daniel Boone, the legendary frontier hero who helped blaze a trail over the Appalachian Mountains into Kentucky for some of the first colonists moving west, was once asked if he had ever been lost. "No, I can't say as ever I was lost, but I was *bewildered* once for three days,"[9] was his savvy, homespun reply.

Boone was one of the frontiersmen known as "long hunters" for their lengthy trips to hunt and explore unknown territory. Their daring, skill, fortitude, and love of adventure led them to brave the wilderness and pave the way for settlers who followed. Boone was born November 2, 1734, in Berks County, Pennsylvania, and his English Quaker family moved to the North Carolina frontier when he was a youngster. He first explored Kentucky in 1769, and he died September 26, 1820, in Missouri, another untamed area he helped settle as an old man.

Although he did not discover the Cumberland Gap, a natural notch in the Appalachian Mountains near the juncture of present-day Virginia, Tennessee, and Kentucky, Boone in 1773 became the first to lead settlers through it into the land that would become Kentucky. Two years later he helped create the Wilderness Road, en- abling establishment of new communities like Boonesboro and settlement of the wild frontier area.

Boone's enthusiastic descriptions of the virgin land he explored helped lure colonists westward: "I returned home to my family [after his first journey through the Cumberland Gap], with a determination to bring them as soon as possible to live in Kentucky, which I esteemed a second paradise, at the risk of my life and my fortune."[10]

EARLY MOVES WEST

The first English settlers stayed close to the Atlantic Ocean, their lifeline to vital supplies from the Old World, but as their numbers grew they needed more and more land. The colonial population boom was due to natural increase and a steady flow of immigrants from England, Germany, France, Scotland, Ireland, and Holland that by 1750 had swelled the thirteen colonies to 1.5 million people.

In 1759 St. John de Crevecoeur, a French immigrant who became a farmer in New York, claimed the new political freedom and economic opportunities colonists enjoyed had transformed their basic character:

> The rich stay in Europe, it is only the middling and poor that emigrate. Everything tends to regenerate them; new law, a new mode of living, a new social system. A European, when he first arrives, seems limited in his intentions as well as his views; but he very suddenly alters his scale. He no sooner breathes our air than he forms new schemes, and embarks on designs he never would have thought of in his own country. He begins to feel the effects of a sort of resurrection; hitherto he had not lived, but simply vegetated; he now feels himself a man. He begins to forget his former servitude and dependence and those new thoughts mark an American. [11]

Great Britain never considered colonization beyond the Allegheny or Appalachian Mountains, which formed a natural geographic barrier, and in 1744 prohibited such settlement through the Quebec Act. But as Lord Dartmouth, secretary of state for the colonies before the Revolutionary War, admitted a decade later, no authority could restrain "that dangerous spirit of unlicensed emigration" [12] that seemed inbred in Americans who kept heading west despite the decree.

These early adventurers had to battle for control of the new lands not only with

Major General Edward Braddock led English troops and colonial militia during the French and Indian War.

DANIEL BOONE: LURING PEOPLE TO THE WILDERNESS

In 1782, when John Filson published a book to convince people to move to Kentucky, he included a section titled "The Adventures of Col. Daniel Boone." Boone's alleged autobiography was actually written by Filson, and is quoted in David Colbert's Eyewitness to the American West.

"We found everywhere abundance of wild beasts of all sorts, through this vast forest [along the Red River]. The buffalo were more frequent than I have seen cattle in the settlements, browsing on the leaves of the cane, or cropping the herbage on those extensive plains, fearless, because ignorant, of the violence of men. Sometimes we saw hundreds in a drove, and the numbers about the salt springs were amazing. We had passed through a great forest, on which stood myriads of trees, some gay with blossoms, others rich with fruits. Nature was here a series of wonder, and a fund of delight. We were diverted with innumerable animals presenting themselves perpetually to our view.

I was surrounded with plenty in the midst of want. I was happy in the midst of dangers and inconveniences. In such a diversity it was impossible I should be disposed to melancholy. No popular city, with all the varieties of commerce and stately structures, could afford so much pleasure to my mind, as the beauties of nature I found here."

An aging Daniel Boone poses with his trusty flintlock rifle. The horn dangling around his waist contains gunpowder.

Indians but with the French and Spanish who had already been there more than a century. The Spaniards reached modern-day Florida as early as 1513 and New Mexico in 1540, and the French began exploring the Mississippi River valley in 1673.

In the mid-eighteenth century, France, England's traditional enemy, controlled most of Canada, which it called New France, as well as the wilderness bordering British possessions south of the Great Lakes. As English colonists advanced into French territory, a series of military clashes began that culminated in the French and Indian War from 1754 to 1763.

The war, which got its name from the many Indians who allied themselves with the French, was fought to determine which nation would settle the upper Ohio River valley. The two nations battled in Europe as well as the contested frontier areas before Great Britain finally prevailed. The 1763 Treaty of Paris gave the victorious British ownership of Canada and everything east of the Mississippi River except New Orleans, a valuable port city controlled by Spain.

New land was now open, and by the end of 1765 some two thousand families, mostly squatters without legal title to holdings, had settled along the forks of the Ohio River near Fort Pitt, which became the city known today as Pittsburgh, Pennsylvania, and by 1780 over ten thousand families were living in that area. The Wilderness Road hacked out by Boone became a gateway to Kentucky and Tennessee, and by 1770 about five thousand settlers had crossed the Appalachian Mountains.

In 1763 Benjamin Franklin exulted over victory in the French and Indian War and boldly predicted, "All the country from the St. Lawrence to the Mississippi will in another century be filled with British people."[13] His prediction was correct, but they would be citizens of the United States, not Great Britain.

A NEW NATION IS BORN

The underlying cause of the Revolutionary War (1775–1783) was that Americans, as British colonists had begun to call themselves, believed they had a right to govern themselves. In the decade after the French and Indian War, Great Britain sowed the seeds of revolution by imposing new taxes to build up a treasury depleted to defend the colonies and by taking a stronger role in governing its growing New World empire.

But colonists resented the new, heavy-handed interference with their affairs, refused to pay new taxes on tea and other merchandise, and ignored orders to halt settlement west of the Appalachians. King George III made Americans even angrier when he sent more soldiers to make them submit to his rule, and the Revolution started April 19, 1775, when British and colonial soldiers fought the Battle of Lexington and Concord.

When the peace treaty ending the war was signed September 3, 1783, the new nation included a vast, unsettled area that extended west to the Mississippi River. Britain still retained Canada but was forced to return East and West Florida to

Colonial rebels exchange fire with British troops in the Battle of Lexington, which helped ignite the American Revolution.

Spain, territories it received after the French and Indian War because Spain fought on the side of France.

Although Americans were victorious in battle, Dr. Benjamin Rush knew the work of creating a new nation had only just begun. One of the signers of the Declaration of Independence in 1776, he wrote, "There is nothing more common than to confound the terms of the American Revolution with the late American War. The American War is over; but that is far from the case with the American Revolution. On the contrary, nothing but the first act of that great drama is closed." [14]

Rush knew that America needed to complete the Revolution by learning to govern itself, and one of the young na-

tion's prickliest problems was how to settle the untamed wilderness bordering the original colonies. Before the war various states had argued over ownership of the new lands, with some claiming their borders extended westward all the way to the Pacific Ocean. The states now surrendered those rights to the federal government, but the problem still remained of how to organize these vast new holdings.

The answer lay in the Northwest Ordinances which Congress passed in 1787 and 1789. Adopted as a plan for orderly settlement and growth in the Northwest Territory—the frontier lying west of Pennsylvania, north of the Ohio River, east of the Mississippi River, and south of the Great Lakes—the Ordinances called for three stages of development before a frontier area could become a state.

Congress first created a "territory" and appointed a governor and judges to make laws that were subject to congressional veto. When the territory's population reached five thousand, citizens were allowed to elect a legislature that would make its own laws. When the population topped sixty thousand, the territory was eligible to become a state equal in rights to the original thirteen.

By 1858 the Northwest Territory would yield five states—Illinois, Indiana, Michigan, Wisconsin, and Ohio. The lasting importance of the Northwest Ordinances was that they provided a mechanism for orderly development of all the states, even far-off Hawaii, which in 1959 became the fiftieth state.

AMERICANS RUSH WEST

Even during the Revolutionary War, settlers had continued to migrate west over the Wilderness Road. Lured by the promise of cheap land—one hundred acres for ten shillings—by the spring of 1780 more than fifty-five thousand settlers had crossed the mountains into Tennessee and Kentucky. Seeing the throngs of migrating colonists, one observer noted "there is Hundreds Traveling hundreds of Miles, they know not what for nor whither, except it's to Kentucky . . . the Land of Milk and Honey." [15]

The end of the war released a new wave of settlers: soldiers given free land for fighting for their country, citizens fleeing postwar economic problems, and immigrants. By 1790 more than 2.25 million people, one-third of the U.S. population, lived west of the mountain ranges that had once held them back. Infected with "Ohio fever," the opportunity to acquire cheap land, settlers poured into the Northwest Territory, Kentucky, and Tennessee. By 1800, Ohio alone had more than forty-five thousand residents. Kentucky became the fifteenth state in 1792, Tennessee was granted statehood four years later, and Ohio joined the Union in 1803.

Settlers struggle through a rugged mountain pass to the lush valley and flowing river below, where they will make their home.

MAKING A HOME IN THE WILDERNESS

It was not easy for pioneer families to make a new home in the wilderness. In The United States to 1865, *historian Michael Kraus sums up the difficulties these hardy pioneers encountered.*

"Clearing the land was the first task of the settler, once he had built his cabin. Corn was planted toward the end of May and in three months or so green, unripe roasting ears were ready. During the summer the frontier family fed on the small quantity of grain carried with them, and the abundant fish and game of the forest. Improvident settlers sometimes exhausted their supply of meal before their new corn was ready.

[As one pioneer recalled:] For that length of time we had to live without bread. The stomach seemed to be always empty, and tormented with a sense of hunger. I remember how the children watched the growth of the potato tops, pumpkin and squash vines, hoping from day to day to get something to [take] the place of bread. How delicious was the taste of the young potatoes when we got them!"

Settlers trim away the wilderness to make a new home in Minnesota.

Although some pioneers claimed frontier land was so rich it needed "only to be tickled with the hoe to laugh with the harvest,"[16] people moving west endured great hardships to carve new homes from the wilderness. In addition to the danger of attacks by Indians who resented whites invading their land, settlers had to clear land for planting, build houses, and quickly grow crops to avoid starving to death their first winter.

The reason they willingly endured such hardship is summed up in an entry Richard Butler made in his journal in 1784 while traveling through Kentucky:

> Here are the finest and most excellent sites for farms, cities, and towns. Here may the industrious and broken-hearted farmer, tired with the slavery of the unfortunate situation in which he was born, lay down his burthen [burden] and find rest on these peaceful and plenteous plains; here may [European immigrants] pour out their superabundant sons and daughters, who with cheerful hearts, and industrious hands will wipe away the tear of tyrannic toil, and join the children of America in the easy labors of comfort and plenty. [17]

By the early 1790s, restless, adventurous settlers were already leaving Kentucky and Tennessee in search of even more fertile land. They began moving into the Mississippi Gulf region, Spanish territory that included East Florida, West Florida, and Louisiana. This was a huge area extending west from the Mississippi River to the Rocky Mountains that would eventually became all or parts of fifteen states, including present-day Louisiana. As Americans kept pushing inland, the Mississippi River, America's western boundary, became an increasingly vital artery of trade and commerce.

Americans needed the mighty river for travel, to transport goods to the seaport of New Orleans for sale, and as a conduit for supplies. In the first years of the 1800s, when it appeared New Orleans might be closed to Americans, President Thomas Jefferson took steps to keep the port open that would, by a twist of fate, result in the nation doubling in size.

The Louisiana Purchase

America's first westward-thinking president, Jefferson had long envisioned a time "when our rapid multiplication will expand itself and cover the whole northern, if not the southern continent." [18] Although Spain owned the Louisiana Territory, it had a minimal presence, and Jefferson did not fear future competition from Spain.

The situation changed drastically on October 15, 1802, when Spain ceded Louisiana back to France, which had owned the area until the treaty ending the French and Indian War in 1763 forced it to surrender the territory. Because the United States and France had been at odds for many years over various issues, Jefferson became concerned that France would close New Orleans to Americans.

To ensure continued access to this vital port, in early 1803 Jefferson ordered French ambassador Robert Livingston to offer to

HOW THE NATION GREW: STATEHOOD DATES

September 3, 1783
The original 13 colonies become the United States of America. They are Connecticut, Delaware, Georgia, Maryland, Massachusetts, New Hampshire, New Jersey, New York, North Carolina, Pennsylvania, Rhode Island, South Carolina, and Virginia.

March 4, 1791	Vermont
June 1, 1792	Kentucky
June 1, 1796	Tennessee
March 1, 1803	Ohio
April 30, 1812	Louisiana
December 11, 1816	Indiana
December 10, 1817	Mississippi
December 3, 1818	Illinois
December 14, 1819	Alabama
March 15, 1820	Maine
August 10, 1821	Missouri
June 15, 1836	Arkansas
January 26, 1837	Michigan
March 3, 1845	Florida
December 29, 1845	Texas
December 28, 1846	Iowa
May 29, 1848	Wisconsin
September 9, 1850	California
May 11, 1858	Minnesota
February 14, 1859	Oregon
January 29, 1861	Kansas
June 19, 1863	West Virginia
October 31, 1864	Nevada
March 1, 1867	Nebraska
August 1, 1876	Colorado
November 2, 1889	North Dakota
November 2, 1889	South Dakota
November 8, 1889	Montana
November 11, 1889	Washington
July 3, 1890	Idaho
July 10, 1890	Wyoming
January 4, 1896	Utah
January 16, 1907	Oklahoma
January 6, 1912	New Mexico
February 14, 1912	Arizona
January 3, 1959	Alaska
August 21, 1959	Hawaii

buy New Orleans. When Livingston began negotiations in France on April 11, a French official surprised him by asking, "What will you give for the whole of Louisiana?" When a shocked Livingston suggested $4 million, the official told him the offer was "too low" but then said, "Reflect and see me tomorrow."[19]

French emperor Napoleon Bonaparte was willing to sell the vast territory because he needed money to fight Great Britain. The Louisiana Purchase was one of history's greatest bargains; for $15 million the United States doubled in size by acquiring 820,000 square miles of territory. When the two countries signed the deal on May 2, 1803, Napoleon admitted he had a second objective in making the sale. "The acquisition of territory," he said, "forever assures the boundaries of the United States. I have just given England a maritime rival who sooner or later will humble its pride." [20]

Americans were joyous a vast new area had been opened for settlement. The only thing they forgot, as always, was that other people already lived there.

THE FIRST AMERICANS

When Christopher Columbus sailed to the New World in 1492, he mistakenly named Native Americans "Indians"; he thought he had landed on the coast of Asia and that they were from India. Although the explorer was wrong, the name survives even today. The Native Americans the first English settlers encountered were descendants of people who had migrated to North America during the Ice Age as much as twenty-five thousand years earlier, when a land bridge connected Asia and Alaska. By 1500 about 1 to 2 million people were living in what would become the United States.

Most tribes welcomed the colonists and helped them learn to adapt to life in their new home. In 1607 Powhatan, an Algonquian chief who headed a confederacy of some thirty-two tribes numbering nearly ten thousand people, befriended the founders of Jamestown, Virginia, teaching them how to grow native corn (maize) and hunt game. In 1620 when the Pilgrims landed at Plymouth Rock on the Massachusetts coast, Squanto, another Algonquian, helped them survive their first difficult winter.

The English responded to this generous hospitality by treating Native Americans as an inferior, uncivilized race, one that should be happy to be ruled by King James I. But when Virginia colonists wanted to crown Powhatan a "subject king," he bristled at the slight to his own power. "I also am a king and this is my land," Powhatan declared. "Your father [king] is to come to me, not I to him." [21]

By the time of Powhatan's death in 1618, Virginians were seizing large chunks of Indian land to grow tobacco, which had become a profitable crop. Four years later this lust for land led to war when the confederacy's new chief, Opechancanough, Powhatan's older brother, attacked Jamestown and killed 347 of its 1,200 residents. Intermittent warfare ensued for fourteen years before British forces aided by Christianized Indians defeated the confederacy.

Pocahontas: Fact and Myth

Some historical figures become so cloaked in myth through time that most of what people know about them is false. In The Shaping of the American Past: To 1877, *Robert Kelley sets the facts straight about the Indian woman Pocahontas, daughter of Algonquian Chief Powhatan, whose personal story reveals how the English came to view Native Americans as an obstacle standing in the way of riches.*

"To force Powhatan to release hostages [taken during sporadic fighting], the colonists captured Pocahontas in 1613 and took her to Jamestown, where she was treated with courtesy and converted to Christianity. John Rolfe was soon in love with her, and she with him. Governor Thomas Dale sought to dissuade Rolfe from marriage: 'Pocahontas,' he said, 'is of a different and despised color; of a hated race, not one of whom has ever looked [to be] above the meanest of the Colonists.'

[The couple married anyway in 1614 and two years later went to England where] Pocahontas was treated as a princess, entertained 'with festivall, state and pompe' and presented to the king and queen. She had a son, Thomas, but the Rolfes were hardly on the boat for their return [to Jamestown] when she sickened and died.

[When tobacco became a valuable crop, relations between colonists and Indians worsened as colonist started taking more land to grow it.] In 1622 the Indians struck back: In a great massacre perhaps a third of the colonists were killed, including John Rolfe. Thereafter, Indians and whites drew apart. A policy of 'perpetual enmity' toward the Indians was adopted."

The authors of *The Americans: The History of a People and a Nation* write that the first encounters between whites and Indians set the tone for future relations:

In general, the Indians first received the colonists on their shores with great curiosity, then with warm friendliness. Time and again, entire settlements such as Jamestown and Plymouth were saved from starvation by the Algonquins. If they had wished, they could have killed the colonists or forced them to flee back to their boats and the sea. It was only after unmistakable signs of settlers intending to take over their land that the Indians became aroused to their danger. By then it was too late. Despite brief but bloody wars, the colonists had too many beachheads on the continent. They were backed up by seemingly unending supplies of people and material from Europe. [22]

As the number of colonists continued to increase, their superior weapons—guns and cannon against bows and arrows, knives, and tomahawks—helped them push tribe after tribe off their ancestral lands. When it was convenient, colonists bought land by promising to pay chiefs a small amount of money each year or by giving them steel knives, cloth, guns, and other items the Indians could not manufacture.

Historian Bernard De Voto believes the desire for such trade goods was key to the downfall of Native Americans:

> The first step in the white man's exploitation of the Indian, and it was the inevitably fatal step, was to raise his standard of living. From the moment when the Indians first encountered manufactured goods they became increasingly dependent on them. Everything in their way of life now pivoted on the acquisition of goods. [23]

Colonists often took advantage of the naïveté of Indians, securing huge tracts of land for materials worth only a few hundred or thousand dollars. President Jefferson, for example, advised citizens to sell things to them even if the Indians did not have any money. "When these debts get beyond what the individuals can pay," Jefferson explained, "they become willing to pay them off by a cession of lands." [24]

But not all Indians gave up their land without a fight.

NATIVE AMERICANS FIGHT BACK

"I mean to destroy the English and leave not one upon our lands,"[25] Chief Pontiac declared on May 7, 1763. The Ottawa chief

This antique print depicts Native Americans attacking a white settlement. The two sides fought for more than a century for control of land that composes the United States.

organized Great Lakes tribes including the Huron, Delaware, Shawnee, Ojibwa, Potawatomi, Miami, Seneca, and Kickapoo and led them in the rebellion known as Pontiac's War (1763–1764). Pontiac won several early battles, captured almost all of the British forts in the Great Lakes area, and made it unsafe for further settlement of Indian lands before British and frontier soldiers defeated his forces.

As more and more Americans pushed into the Ohio Country after the Revolutionary War, other tribes fought back against the white invaders. In May 1791, General Charles Scott issued this stern warning to Indians living north of the Ohio River, where resistance was the fiercest:

> [The United States] has no desire to destroy the red people, although they have the power; should you decline this invitation, and pursue your unprovoked hostilities, their strength will be exerted against you; your warriors will be slaughtered, your villages ransacked and destroyed, your wives and children carried into captivity, and you may be assured that those who escape the fury of our mighty chiefs, shall find no resting place on this side of the Great Lakes.[26]

Despite his threat, Indians for several years were victorious over troops trying to subdue them. But on August 20, 1794, General Anthony Wayne ended the insurrection with a major victory at the Battle of Fallen Timbers in northwestern Ohio. The defeated tribes had to sign the Treaty of Greenville, which forced them to accept a token ten thousand dollars for the southern two-thirds of the area between Lake Erie and the Ohio River. This opened up settlement of land that included two-thirds of modern-day Ohio, part of Indiana, and other areas in the Northwest Territory.

In 1802 the Shawnee complained that white settlers were taking so much of their land in Georgia and killing so much game that it was becoming difficult to feed themselves: "Stop your people from killing our game. They would be angry if we were to kill a cow or hog of theirs. The little game that remains is very dear to us."[27]

But for the next century, American Indian policy would be based on the belief that Native Americans had no right to the lands they controlled because whites could put it to better use. James Monroe summed up this theory when he became president in 1817: "The hunter or savage states require a greater extent of territory to sustain it than is compatible with the progress and just claims of civilized life, and must yield to it."[28]

This clash of cultures would result in decades of brutal warfare between Indians and whites.

Chapter

2 Pushing the Frontier to the Pacific Ocean

President Thomas Jefferson sent Congress a secret message on January 18, 1803, requesting approval for an expedition to explore the continent west to the Pacific Ocean. It was an idea born of the desire Jefferson had held since he was a small boy, one still burning brightly, to know more about the mysterious frontier.

The mission took on added importance later that year when the Louisiana Purchase made that vast tract of land part of the United States. To head his Corps of Discovery, Jefferson chose Captain Meriwether Lewis, who was his private secretary, and Lieutenant William Clark, a veteran of the Indian wars and longtime friend of Lewis.

Numbering some forty men, the Corps started up the Missouri River in three boats on May 14, 1804. After more than a year of arduous, hazardous travel over rivers, plains, and the Rocky Mountains, on November 15, 1805, they reached the mouth of the Columbia River, which flows into the Pacific Ocean. After wintering with a friendly band of Clatsop Indians, they began their long trip home, returning to St. Louis on September 23, 1806.

One of the most thrilling sagas of American exploration, this epic journey helped map and provide detailed information about an area that seemed as strange and unknown to Americans then as the moon and distant planets. Lewis and Clark both wrote fact-filled reports, although Clark's were riddled with spelling mistakes. Early in the journey he noted that "muskeetors [mosquitoes are] very troublesome" and later commented that some large trees that must have been knocked down by "a Dreddfull harican [dreadful hurricane]." [29]

In *Meriwether Lewis: A Biography*, author Richard A. Dillon claims Americans owe a lasting debt to Lewis because the expedition helped interest Americans in the far-off frontier:

> If any one man deserves to be considered as the person who opened the Far West, it is Lewis. With William Clark, he led the way through a terra incognita and proved the feasibility of transcontinental travel. [30]

THE FUR TRADE

Fur trappers were the first to make practical use of the Lewis and Clark data; their reports of a land teeming with beaver and other furbearing animals ignited a new era in the fur industry the French and British had first begun in the seventeenth century. American and English ships had been sailing to the Pacific Northwest since the late eighteenth century to trade for furs, which they exchanged in China for sandalwood and other goods to sell at home.

SACAGAWEA: THE NEW U.S. DOLLAR COIN HONORS HER

The one-dollar coin that debuted in 2000 bears the image of Sacagawea, a young woman who played an important role in the Lewis and Clark expedition. Her ability to communicate with other Native Americans helped the expedition succeed in reaching the Pacific Ocean. The U.S. Mint has written this explanation of Sacagawea's contributions:

". . . Her contribution far exceeded anything Lewis and Clark had bargained for. She provided crucial knowledge of the topography of some of the most rugged country of North America and taught the explorers how to find edible roots and plants previously unknown to European-Americans. With her infant son bound to her back, she single-handedly rescued Captain Clark's journals from the Missouri whitewater when their boat capsized. If she had not, much of the record of the first year of the expedition would have been lost.

Most crucially, however, Sacagawea and her infant served as a 'white flag' of peace for the expedition. They entered potentially hostile territory well armed but undermanned compared to Native American tribes they met. Because no war party was ever accompanied by a woman and infant, the response of the Native Americans was curiosity, not aggression. They talked first, and Sacagawea often served as the translator. Not a single member of the party was lost to hostile action."

Sacagawea proved to be a valuable asset to the Lewis and Clark expedition.

In 1808, New York City furrier John Jacob Astor started the American Fur Company, establishing a string of posts in the Northwest, including Astoria at the mouth of the Columbia River. By 1834, when Astor sold his interest in the business, the firm and its subsidiaries had become the nation's wealthiest company. In the mid-1820s the rising popularity of dress hats made from plush beaver fur sent hundreds of Americans streaming into the Rocky Mountains and was responsible for the following ad in St. Louis newspapers on March 20, 1822: "To Enterprising Young Men: The subscriber wishes to engage ONE HUNDRED MEN to ascend the river Missouri to its source, there to be employed for one, two or three years. For particulars enquire of Major Andrew Henry or to Wm. H. Ashley." [31]

Henry and Ashley were recruiting trappers for their new Rocky Mountain Fur Company, which for the next two decades challenged Astor and French and English firms during one of the most colorful chapters in America's Westward Expansion. One of the first trappers was John Colter, a member of the Lewis and Clark expedition who went back to the Rocky Mountains shortly after returning home from that first long, incredible journey to the Pacific.

Legendary mountain men like Jim Bridger, Joe Meek, Kit Carson, Jedediah Smith, William Sublette, Peter Skene Ogden, and James Beckwourth endured tremendous hardships and danger, living in secluded mountain areas all winter to trap beaver so dandies back east could parade in top-hatted finery. They faced the constant threat of attack from Indians, mainly the Blackfoot, the northwestern plains' strongest, most aggressive tribe and sworn enemy of all whites. Even the Crow, who were friendly to trappers, sometimes stole their horses and supplies.

Most trappers made only enough to reequip themselves for another season, but they gloried in their freedom and the chance to travel where no one but Native Americans ever had. One trapper said "to explore unknown regions was [my] chief delight." [32] These hardy, daring mountain men ranged over a vast, unmapped wilderness of more than a million square miles, locating and mapping mountain passes and trails to the Northwest, Southwest, and the Pacific Ocean that pioneers would use decades later.

In *America's Western Frontiers: The Exploration and settlement of the Trans-Mississippi West*, John A. Hawgood claims the nation owes these colorful characters a huge debt:

> In his few allotted years the trapper set his impress forever upon the map of the nation and the fate of the United States. He affected the destiny of nations; he changed the future of a continent; he bequeathed to later generations of America a tradition of heroic exploration comparable to that of the season of Elizabeth or the conquistadors of Spain. [33]

Bridger, at first mistakenly believing he had reached the Pacific Ocean, was the first white to view the Great Salt Lake. In 1824 at South Pass, Smith was the first non-Native to cross the Rockies, a key part of the Oregon Trail that pioneers took to California and Oregon, and he led a party from the Great Salt Lake to California across miles of desert in what is now Arizona. David Jackson and Sublette were the first non-Natives to view the Yellowstone River and its unusual natural phenomena like the geysers. Their

MOUNTAIN MAN RENDEZVOUS

In the spring the mountain men who trapped beaver headed to a designated spot to sell their furs and buy supplies. One of these annual gatherings was described by writer Washington Irving in his 1837 book The Adventures of Captain Bonneville.

"From the middle of June to the middle of September all trapping is suspended, for the beavers are then shedding their furs and their skins are of little value. This, then, is the trappers holiday, when he is all for fun and frolic and ready for a saturnalia among the mountains. They drank together, they sang, they laughed, they whooped; they tried to outbrag and outlie each other in stories of their adventures and achievements. Here the trappers were in all their glory; they consider themselves the 'cocks of the walk' and always carried the highest crest. Now and then familiarity was pushed too far and would effervesce into a brawl and a rough-and-tumble fight; but it all ended in cordial reconciliation and maudlin endearment."

A mountain man pauses at a stream as he journeys to the nearest trading post.

explorations are commemorated today by places that bear their names—a mountain pass, river, and city in Nevada are named after Carson, a city in Utah is named after Ogden, and a pass in the Sierra Nevada mountain range is named for Beckwourth.

Beckwourth was an African American who went west to escape racist treatment. On the frontier, people tended to judge others by their actions, not the color of their skin, and Beckwourth was a competent, reliable wilderness companion. In his autobiography, he writes of finding Beckwourth Pass:

> I had come to discover what I suspected to be a pass. It was the latter end of April when we entered upon an extensive valley at the northwest extremity of the Sierra range. Swarms of wild bees and ducks were swimming on the surface of the cool crystal stream or sailed the air in clouds over our heads. Deer and antelope filled the plains, and their boldness was conclusive that the hunter's rifle was to them unknown. Nowhere visible were any traces of the white man's approach, and it is probable that our steps were the first [besides Indians] that ever marked the spot. [34]

In 1829 the *St. Louis Beacon* noted that a group Sublette headed to take supplies to the Wind River area in the Rockies was the first to cross the plains with wagons. The paper boasted:

> The ease with which they did it and [the fact they] could have gone on

Washington Irving shortly before his death. This noted American author was fascinated by the rugged mountain men.

[through South Pass] to the mouth of the Columbia, shows the folly and nonsense of those "scientific" characters who talk of the Rocky Mountains as the barrier which will stop the westward march of the American people. [35]

The mountain men caught the imagination of many Americans including Washington Irving, the famed author of *Rip Van Winkle* and *The Legend of Sleepy Hollow*, who in the 1830s left the safety of New York City to tour the Rockies and meet the adventurers he admired and envied. "There was no class of men on the face of the earth," exclaimed Irving, "who lead a life of more continued exertion, peril, and excitement than the trappers of the West." [36]

This fascinating era ended abruptly in the mid-1840s when another turn in fashion tastes, this time toward silk top hats, ended the demand for beaver pelts.

SETTLEMENT CONTINUES

Glowing reports by Lewis and Clark, trappers, and others of the natural riches of the Pacific Coast began to interest Americans in the Oregon Country—the area that extended from California to Alaska and from the Rocky Mountains to the Pacific Ocean—as well as neighboring California, then a Spanish colony.

But in the first three decades of the nineteenth century, Americans were not willing to trek cross-country to find a new home. They were too busy taming the frontier that lay much closer as they pushed west and south into the Northwest Territory and the vast new lands acquired in the Louisiana Purchase.

George Flower was an Englishman who settled on the Illinois prairie around 1815. He wrote that the driving force behind the continuing westward movement and chief glory of every American was the chance to own land, a privilege only members of royalty or the wealthy enjoyed in Europe.

> The practical liberty of America is found in its great space and small population. Good land, dog-cheap everywhere, and for nothing, if you will go for it, gives as much elbow room to every man as he chooses to take. Poor laborers, from every country in Europe, hear of this cheap land, are attracted to it. They come, they toil, they prosper. This is the real liberty of America. [37]

Between 1810 and 1820 the population north of the Ohio River more than doubled and within the next decade the Ohio Valley drew nearly a million settlers, a population greater than that of Massachusetts and Connecticut combined. Louisiana was admitted to the union in 1812 and within a decade five more states were added—Indiana (1816), Mississippi (1817), Illinois (1818), Alabama (1819), and Missouri (1821).

Newspapers recorded the westward drive as it streamed past the doors of their offices. *The Detroit Gazette* on March 21, 1823, reported that "for a few days past our wharves and taverns have been literally thronged with people emigrating to this new country [Michigan], nearly all of whom appear to belong to the most valuable class of settlers—practical farmers, of moderate capital and good habits." [38]

Despite the rapid growth, it was not easy making a new home in the wilderness. Elizabeth Clemmons Smith, who moved with her family from North Carolina to Pike County, Illinois, in 1821, wrote of one of the perils pioneers encountered—wild animals:

> Wolves and panthers were destructive to our stock. I have carried a gun on more than one occasion to assist

the killing of wolves that were after our stock. I was chased by a panther nearly a mile, taking refuge in an old cabin. When I had just closed the door, it sprang upon the roof and I had to remain there all night. [39]

EXPANSIONIST POLICY

In addition to running into resistance from Native Americans as they moved west, Americans early in the nineteenth century had to contend with other nations that wielded power in various parts of the continent. Spain controlled California, East and West Florida, and the Southwest from Texas to California; Great Britain still disputed the border between Canada and the United States; and Britain, Spain, and Russia all claimed the Oregon Country.

Historian Frederick Jackson Turner writes that after America first won its freedom, President George Washington did not believe the young nation was strong enough to contend with other countries: "It was Washington's objective that the new nation should grow and thrive in peace until the strength of union was a reality and a just and powerful United States could assume its rightful position among the nations of the worlds." [40]

But after what Washington called a "necessary breathing spell of peace," [41] the United States in the nineteenth century began to assert itself as it grew in size, population, and economic power. And the strongest calls for action to eliminate competition on the continent from other nations came from frontier citizens who lusted after yet more new land. The first step the United States took in this direction was declaring the War of 1812 against Great Britain.

The relationship between the two nations, strained at best since the Revolutionary War, worsened in the early 1800s. Americans were angry that British ships dared to stop U.S. vessels to search for deserters from the English navy or to seize shipments bound for France, its bitter enemy. There was a growing animosity against England because it disputed the official boundary between the United States and Canada and challenged Americans for land they believed should belong to the United States. Worst of all, Americans knew British traders and soldiers were arming Indians and supporting them in their battle against U.S. settlers. Historian Sanford Wexler claims

> the second military clash with Great Britain was a Westerners' war. It was those in the Northwest [Territory] who demanded the conquest of Canada; those in the Southwest and South who called for the seizure of Florida from Spain. They encouraged the war and helped it become a reality. [42]

Seventy new congressmen were elected in 1810, many of them known as "War Hawks" for their belligerent attitude toward Great Britain. On June 1, 1812, when President James Madison, himself an ardent expansionist, asked Congress to declare war on Great Britain, the War Hawks were only too happy to say yes. Rep. John C. Calhoun of South Carolina proudly declared the "sons of America [would]

President James Madison asked Congress to declare war on Great Britain. In 1814 the British seized Washington and set fire to the executive mansion.

prove to the World that we have not only inherited the liberty which our Fathers gave us, but also the will and power to maintain it." [43]

Unfortunately, the United States was woefully unprepared for war; it had only a half-dozen warships and a trained army of just sixty-seven hundred men. When an attempted U.S. invasion of Canada ended in utter defeat, the Northwest Territory was thrown open to attack by Indian tribes, who viewed the war as a golden opportunity to strike back at settlers.

Leading the way was the great Shawnee chief, Tecumseh.

TECUMSEH: THE GREAT INDIAN LEADER

In 1810 when Governor William Henry Harrison ordered the removal of all Indians from the Indiana Territory, Tecumseh rose up to oppose him. Tecumseh, who with his brother, the Prophet, had fought white settlement of the Ohio River basin for many years, rallied Great Lakes tribes for an all-out war. In a speech to assembled tribes in October 1811, Tecumseh declared:

> Let the white race perish! They seize your land, they corrupt your women, they trample on the grass of your dead. Back whence they came, upon a trail of blood, they must be driven. Burn their houses, destroy their stock! The red man owns the country and the palefaces must never enjoy it. War now, war forever! [44]

Tecumseh led a series of devastating attacks that temporarily halted new settlement. When the War of 1812 began, Tecumseh allied himself with the British and was commissioned a brigadier general. "Here is a chance such as will never occur again," he said, "for the Indians of North America to form ourselves in one great combination." [45]

Tecumseh traveled extensively to recruit tribes for the British, which was not an easy task according to historian Jon E. Lewis: "The Indians did not see themselves as a homogeneous entity, just as Europeans do not see themselves as alike, but as English, French, or German." [46]

This lack of unity hurt Native Americans throughout their century-long fight against white expansion. When a combined British and Indian force was defeated October 5, 1813, at the Battle of the Thames in southern Canada, Tecumseh was killed.

THE UNITED STATES TRIUMPHS

After the failed invasion of Canada, Great Britain retaliated and British troops in August 1814 briefly captured the nation's capital, setting fire to the White House in the process. The turning point in the war was a series of victories on sea and then on land by forces led by General Andrew Jackson, a future president who stopped an attempted English invasion through New Orleans.

"Old Hickory," as Jackson was known, achieved his greatest triumph when his army of leather-clad frontiersmen won a smashing victory over red-coated British soldiers in the Battle of New Orleans. The tragedy is that the bloody battle was fought after peace had been declared but before word the war was over reached combatants.

Sir Edward Pakenham, believing that capturing New Orleans could win the war, landed seventy-five hundred troops in the swamps near the city. On the morning of January 8, 1815, he ordered his soldiers to attack the heavily fortified city. Advancing bravely, but foolishly, in solid ranks across open ground, his troops were slaughtered. Historian Carter Smith describes the carnage:

> Firing from cover, the Americans killed or wounded about 2,000 British

Frontiersmen and U.S. soldiers fire a deadly volley of cannon balls and bullets into rows of advancing British troops in the Battle of New Orleans.

soldiers in less than an hour—including Pakenham, who was mortally wounded. The British quickly retreated. With the victory, American control of the Mississippi Valley was secure, and the nation had a new hero, Andrew Jackson. [47]

In the Treaty of Ghent (1814) that ended the war, the British made concessions that solidified the U.S.-Canadian border in favor of the United States. It also put the fate of the Oregon Country on hold by establishing a joint occupation of the area by the United States and Great Britain for at least a decade.

Emboldened by its military success, the United States became aggressive in opposing European interference in what it now perceived to be its own sphere of influence, the continents of North and South America. Because President James Monroe and Secretary of State John Quincy Adams feared European powers still wanted to create new colonies in the Americas, Monroe in 1823 bluntly told them to stay out of the hemisphere.

In a message to Congress in which he outlined what came to known as the Monroe Doctrine, the president noted that the United States had refrained from participating in wars involving European nations. Monroe then warned them that "we should consider any attempt on their part to extend their system to any portion of the Hemisphere as dangerous to our peace and safety."[48] The United States was finally taking a forceful stand in world politics, at least as they related to its own interests at home.

In addition to an upsurge in national pride and confidence, the War of 1812 also had an effect on relations with Native Americans—one that proved disastrous for them.

INDIAN REMOVAL

After the war the United States punished Indian tribes that had fought on the British side by making them sign new treaties that opened huge tracts of Indian land for settlement in the Midwest. The same thing had happened to tribes that had allied themselves with U.S. foes during the French and Indian War and the Revolutionary War.

Waves of settlers began pouring into this new frontier, forcing more Indians off their land. Some tribes tried to fight back, but resistance was futile. In 1832 Chief Black Hawk refused to give up his village at Rock Island, Illinois, and led Sauk and Fox Indians in the brief uprising known as the Black Hawk War. Future president Abraham Lincoln was a captain in the war, which ended with the Battle of Bad Axe on the Mississippi River in present-day southwestern Wisconsin.

After being driven relentlessly from their homes and through the wilderness, hundreds of Sauk and Fox men, women, and children were slaughtered when white forces caught them trying to cross the river at Bad Axe. Even one of the frontiersmen who participated in the massacre was appalled: "It was a horrid sight to witness little children, wounded and suffering the most excruciating pain, although they were of the savage enemy." [49]

The federal government soon decided on a policy of Indian removal to give whites total control of the frontier. Between 1817 and 1821 dozens of tribes in the Ohio Valley were forced to live on reservations or move to the wilderness beyond the Mississippi River, which opened up land in the eventual states of Illinois, Indiana, and Michigan.

One of the major figures in this policy was Jackson, a president praised by historians for his belief that average citizens

Chief Black Hawk, who led Sauk and Fox Indians in the ill-fated Black Hawk War. This picture was painted years after the conflict.

TRAIL OF TEARS

When fourteen thousand Cherokee were banished to Oklahoma from their homes in Georgia and Tennessee to make room for white settlers, some four thousand died along the way in what became known as the Trail of Tears. Following is an anonymous account by a white settler who saw the migrating Cherokee. It is taken from David Colbert's Eyewitness to the American West.

[In December 1838 we saw a] "detachment of the poor Cherokee Indians, about eleven hundred Indians—sixty wagons—six hundred horses, and perhaps forty pairs of oxen. We found them in the forest camped for the night by the road side under a severe fall of rain accompanied by heavy wind. With their canvas for a shield from the inclemency of the weather and the cold, wet ground for a resting place, after the fatigue of the day, they spent the night. Many of the aged Indians were suffering extremely from the journey. Several were then quite ill, and an aged man we were informed was then in the last struggles of death.

We met several detachments in the southern part of Kentucky on the 4th, 5th, and 6th of December. The sick and feeble were carried in wagons, a great many ride on horseback and multitudes go on foot, even aged females, apparently nearly ready to drop into the grave, were traveling with heavy burdens attached to the back, on the sometimes frozen ground, and sometimes muddy streets, with no covering for the feet except what nature had given them. We learned from the inhabitants on the road where the Indians passed, that they buried fourteen or fifteen at every stopping place, and they make a journey of ten miles per day only on an average."

had as much right to govern as wealthy or powerful people. But historian Alan Axelrod claims that "even for admirers of the seventh president of the United States, the name of Andrew Jackson is forever linked to the inequitable, immoral, and inhumane federal policy of Indian removal." [50]

The Tennessean, who had fought Indians since his youth, used the War of 1812 as an excuse to seize territory from the Creek Indians, who he believed had no right to control so much land. Although the Creek numbered only eight thousand, they ruled an area of more than 40 million acres, roughly half the size of California. When a group of Creek Indians who became known as Red Sticks responded to Tecumseh's call to help the British, Jackson in 1813 led an army of frontiersmen against them.

With a force that included pro-American White Stick Creek, Jackson scored a decisive victory in the Battle of Horseshoe Bend in March 1814. The White Sticks had become U.S. allies in hopes of keeping their land, but the treaty that resulted seized 23 million acres from the Creek, unfairly punishing White Sticks as well as Red Sticks while pushing the tide of white settlement from the Tennessee River to the Gulf of Mexico. In *The Shaping of the American Past*, Robert Kelley claims the victory is "of towering importance in American history" because

> It sealed the eventual doom of the Five Civilized Nations [the Creek, Chickasaw, Cherokee, Choctaw, and Seminole] by initiating the process of clearing out the Indians and making possible white settlement. It also sharply diverted the course of the War of 1812, which to this point had been a dismal failure for the Americans. [51]

Acting under orders from President James Monroe, in 1818 Jackson led a military expedition into Spanish East Florida on the pretext of punishing Seminole Indians who were raiding U.S. settlements. Instead, Jackson seized a Spanish military installation, executed two British subjects who he accused of inciting the attacks, took over Pensacola, and declared the laws of the United States in effect in East Florida, the area that today encompasses the state of Florida.

Spain was angry but powerless to stop the takeover. In the 1819 Transcontinental Treaty following talks between the two nations, Spain ceded East Florida to the United States and gave up its rights north of California in the Pacific Northwest. The United States in 1810 had already annexed West Florida, a small section on the Gulf of Mexico adjoining East Florida, after claiming that area should have been part of the Louisiana Purchase.

In his role as military commander, Jackson between 1815 and 1820 forced many tribes to sign treaties surrendering territory that today makes up three-fourths of Florida, one-fifth of Georgia and Mississippi, and small parts of North Carolina and Kentucky. When he became president in 1829, Jackson pursued his goal of driving Indians entirely out of the East. In 1830 he helped pass the Indian Removal Act, which forced tribes to move to Indian Territory, a distant frontier area Congress established in what today is Oklahoma. The Cherokee claimed the government had no right to take their land and won a Supreme Court decision in their favor, *Worcester v. Georgia* (1832).

But Jackson ignored the ruling, forcing the Cherokee to move to Oklahoma in 1835. In a journey known as the Trail of Tears, nearly a third of the fourteen thousand Cherokee who walked the twelve hundred miles died of starvation and illness. In his 1837 farewell address, Jackson hypocritically announced he had helped place eastern tribes "beyond the reach of injury or oppression, and that [the] paternal care of the General Government will hereafter watch over them and protect them." [52]

The United States never lived up to that promise.

3 The Lone Star State and the Mormon Migration

Members of the Texas Constitutional Convention were gathered in Washington-on-the-Brazos February 28, 1836, when a dusty rider galloped wildly into the tiny frontier settlement and grimly delivered a note from Lieutenant Colonel William Barret Travis, the twenty-seven-year-old commander of the defenders of the Alamo.

Dated February 24 and addressed "To the People of Texas," Travis reported that he and his small force of 180 were "besieged by a thousand or more of the Mexicans" behind the thick stone walls of the Spanish mission in San Antonio. Despite having endured "a continual Bombardment & Cannonade for 24 hours," Travis vowed not to surrender.

> I call on you in the name of Liberty, or patriotism & everything dear to the American character, to come to our aid with all dispatch. If this call is neglected, I am determined to sustain myself as long as possible. I die like a soldier who never forgets what is due to his own honor & that of his country—VICTORY OR DEATH. [53]

Help did not arrive in time. On March 6 soldiers commanded by Mexican president General Antonio López de Santa Anna breached the mission walls, killing Travis and the survivors of his gallant band who for thirteen days had heroically withstood a far superior force of six thousand.

In dying, however, the defenders gained historic immortality. "Remember the Alamo!" became the war cry that inspired their fellow Texans to win independence from Mexico and begin the U.S. conquest of the Southwest.

THE SPANISH INFLUENCE

Early in the nineteenth century, the United States forced Spain to relinquish its eastern possessions, but Spain still controlled a huge territory in the West, an area it had explored before any other European nation. In 1519 Hernando Cortés and a small band of Spanish soldiers landed at present-day Veracruz on the coast of Mexico. Bernal Díaz del Castillo, the expedition's chronicler, wrote of their amazement when they sighted the magnificent Aztec city of Tenochtitlán: "We said it was like the enchantments they tell of in legends. [There were] great towers and buildings rising from the water, and all built of masonry. And some of our soldiers even asked whether the things we saw were not in a dream." [54]

Aztec emperor Montezuma II threw open the gates of Tenochtitlán, welcoming Cortés and his men because he believed they were gods. But within five years the Spanish conquered the Aztecs, killed Montezuma, and began to forge a vast new empire that included Mexico as well as modern-day California, Texas, New Mexico, Utah, and Arizona.

Despite authoritarian rule and heavy taxes levied by far-off officials, there was little resistance to Spanish rule in Mexico or its provinces before the nineteenth century. But in the early 1800s, in much the same way American colonists had earlier rebelled against the British, Mexican citizens began to seek the right to govern themselves.

After two failed insurrections, a third led by Vicente Guerrero succeeded, and in 1821 Spain granted Mexico its independence. The struggling, bankrupt Republic of Mexico decided that to strengthen itself, it must lure more people to its three distant, lightly populated provinces of Alta California, Nuevo Mexico, and Coahuila-Texas. In 1800 Texas had just three small settlements—San Antonio, Goliad, and Nacogdoches—and only two thousand Mexican citizens, called "Tejanos."

Mexico's offer of free land for anyone willing to move to Texas unleashed a flood of American settlers, who quickly outnumbered the Tejanos and began the process of transforming the sleepy Mexican province into a U.S. possession.

INVITATION TO TEXAS

Moses Austin was born in Connecticut but drifted west to Spanish-owned territory and became a Spanish citizen. When Austin died in June 1821, six months after winning approval from Mexican officials to allow Americans to settle in Texas, his final request was that his twenty-seven-year-old son, Stephen, make the proposed colony a reality. Stephen F. Austin, who once declared "Texas is my mistress,"[55] devoted his life to helping create Texas.

In 1821 Austin began moving three hundred American families to the village

Stephen F. Austin, known as "the father of Texas," brought American families into Mexican territory.

of San Felipe de Austin on the Brazos River. The Old Three Hundred, as they became known, were the first of thousands of Americans who migrated to the vast, empty spaces and began calling themselves "Texians." They came because Mexico offered each new immigrant family both a *sitio* (4,428 acres of pasture for ranching) and a *labor* (177 acres of farmland) under the *empresario* system, in which one person was granted enough land for one hundred families. The chosen *empresario*, or leader, had the responsibility of recruiting settlers to live there.

In 1827, nineteen-year-old Noah Smithwick moved to Texas. He wrote that he left Hopkinsville, Kentucky "with all my worldly possessions, which consisted of a few dollars in money, a change of clothes, and a gun, of course, to seek my fortune in this lazy man's paradise."[56] Smithwick was persuaded to venture to Texas by Sterling C. Robinson, who visited Kentucky in 1826 to recruit settlers. Smithwick wrote that Robinson painted a tantalizing picture of Texas:

> [Texas had] an abundance of game, wild horses, cattle, turkeys, buffalo; deer and antelope by the drove. The woods abounded in bee trees, wild grapes, plums, cherries, persimmons, and dewberries, while walnuts, hickory nuts, and pecans were abundant along the water courses. The climate was so mild that houses were not essential; neither was an abundance of clothing or bedding, buffalo robes and bearskins supplying all that was

needed for the latter and buckskin the former. [57]

Robinson, Smithwick noted, wisely said nothing of the hardships of making a home in the wilderness, danger from hostile Comanche or Apache Indians, or the possibility of a future fight with Mexico over control of the rich new land.

"Gone to Texas" became a popular shorthand phrase to refer to the phenomenal mass migration to this new frontier. By 1830 about twenty thousand Americans had moved there and by 1836 nearly thirty thousand more joined them. Many came as part of the *empresario* system, but hundreds of families simply packed up their belongings, put signs on their homes that read "G. T. T." (Gone to Texas), and blithely crossed the border in search of prosperity.

As Americans began to outnumber the Tejanos, Mexico in 1830 issued an order barring further settlement. But U.S. citizens ignored the edict and kept pouring into Texas to claim free land—a bargain at a time when even cheap wilderness tracts purchased from the U.S. government cost at least $1.25 an acre.

TEXAS REBELLION

As Americans grew in numbers they began to resent being governed by far-off Mexican officials, who they considered corrupt as well as inefficient. The Mexican government, meanwhile, was angry that most new Texans failed to honor two promises they made in return for free land—to become Roman Catholics and citizens of Mexico. Historian Robert Kel-

DAVY CROCKETT DIES AT THE ALAMO

By far the most famous of the 180 men who died at the Alamo was Davy Crockett, the legendary frontiersman and former congressman from Tennessee. After losing his congressional seat because he opposed many of President Andrew Jackson's policies, Crockett decided to go to Texas, arriving in San Antonio in February 1836, just in time to join the defense of the Alamo.

In The Heritage of America, *historians Henry Steele Commager and Allan Nevins cite fragments of a diary Crockett allegedly kept during the siege.*

"February 19—We are all in high spirits, though we are rather short of provisions, for men who have appetites that could digest anything but oppression; but no matter, we have a prospect of soon getting our bellies full of fighting, and that is victuals and drink to a true patriot any day.

February 29—I had a little sport this morning before breakfast. The enemy had planted a [cannon] within gunshot of the fort during the night, and they commenced a brisk cannonade point-blank against the spot where I was snoring. A fellow stepped up to touch her off, but before he could apply the match I let him have it, and he keeled over.

March 3—We have given over all hopes of receiving assistance. Colonel Travis harangued the garrison and concluded by exhorting them, in case the enemy should carry the fort, to fight to the last gasp and render their victory even more serious to them than to us. This was followed by three cheers.

March 4—Shells have been falling into the fort like hail during the day, but without effect.

March 5—Pop, pop, pop! Bom, bom, bom! throughout the day. No time for memorandums now. Go ahead! Liberty and independence forever! [This was Crockett's last entry.]"

ley claims the main reason for the deteriorating relationship was the inability of the two sides to understand each other:

Fundamentally, the Texas revolution arose from an irresolvable conflict of cultures. Many Americans in Texas regarded Mexican ways of life as inferior and debased. Within the province of Texas itself, those of Mexican descent had become a minority group held in contempt. Mexican ways of governing seemed tyrannical and arbitrary. [58]

The final blow came in 1834 when Santa Anna, elected a year earlier as president of Mexico, abolished the republic's

Mexican soldiers engage in combat with defenders of the Alamo. The buckskin-clad fighter wielding his rifle as a club had probably run out of gunpowder.

democratic constitution and assumed the powers of a dictator. Refusing to live under such a system, Texans demanded that their rights under the Mexican constitution be restored.

When Santa Anna entered Texas with a force of several thousand soldiers to quell the rebellion, Texas leaders meeting on March 2, 1836, at Washington-on-the-Brazos declared the province's independence. They chose David G. Burnet interim president of the Republic of Texas, appointed former Tennessee governor Sam Houston military commander, and named Austin commissioner to the United States, with orders to secure strategic aid and enlist army volunteers. But by this time, the fight for independence was already under way.

In late 1835 a detachment of volunteers drove Mexican soldiers out of San Antonio and occupied the old Spanish mission known as the Alamo in a move to slow down Santa Anna's advancing army and give settlers time to organize militarily. Realizing the small force could not withstand Santa Anna, Houston and other leaders advised it to abandon the Alamo. But volunteers including legendary frontiersmen Davy Crockett and James Bowie refused to leave, and on February 23 Santa Anna and his troops began their bloody siege.

The valiant defenders held out for thirteen days before being overwhelmed by some six thousand soldiers, who on the final day stormed through a breach created by cannon fire in the Alamo's tall, thick outer wall. Santa Anna had gone to war carrying a black flag, signifying he would show no mercy to anyone who opposed him. "In this war," Santa Anna said, "there are no prisoners."[59]

When the Alamo fell he spared only about fifteen people, mostly women and children; five defenders still alive were executed, including a wounded Crockett. The defenders of the Alamo, however, had made Santa Anna pay a high price for victory, killing about fifteen hundred soldiers before being defeated.

VICTORY AT SAN JACINTO

Five days after the Alamo fell, Suzanna Dickenson, whose husband died in the fighting, her fifteen-month-old daughter, Angelina, and a servant named Joe located Sam Houston, whose army was camped on the Guadalupe River about seventy miles east of San Antonio. Santa Anna had released Dickenson so she could deliver a message to the upstart Texans: All who rebelled against Mexico would suffer the same fate as the defenders of the Alamo. The Mexican dictator fulfilled that dread warning March 27 after defeating another group of 350 Texans at Goliad; after they surrendered, Santa Anna executed them all.

An officer under Andrew Jackson during the War of 1812, Houston had to find a way to defeat a far larger Mexican force with a ragtag army of some 400 men. Houston decided to retreat before the advancing Mexicans until he could lure them into a favorable spot for a battle. Houston biographer John Hoyt Williams writes:

> The month-long retreat known in Texas as "The Runaway Scrape" was both a military withdrawal and a folk migration, for hundreds of families from communities along the Guadalupe, San Antonio and San Marcos rivers packed what they could in panic and streamed northeast. According to Captain John M. Swisher, an officer with Houston's force, "all the country west of the Brazos was depopulated." [60]

As Texans flocked to the charismatic Houston, his army grew and people began to question why he did not stop running

Sam Houston led Texan forces against the army of Mexican president Santa Anna.

and challenge Santa Anna. Even President Burnet wrote him a stinging letter: "The enemy are laughing you to scorn. You must retreat no more. The country expects you to fight." [61]

When the Texas army camped on April 18, 1836, at Buffalo Bayou just north of Harrisburg, Houston told his dispirited troops, weary of fleeing before the Mexicans, that it was finally time to fight. Santa Anna had trailed them and was camped nearby with nearly 1,000 soldiers, over 200 more men than Houston now commanded. Astride his big white stallion, Saracen, Houston delivered a fiery speech to his buckskin-clad army: "Victory is certain! Trust in God and fear not! The victims of the Alamo and the names of those who were murdered at Goliad cry out for cool, deliberate vengeance. Remember the Alamo! Remember Goliad!"[62]

The next day Houston moved his men across Buffalo Bayou on crude rafts, and they camped near the junction of the bayou and the San Jacinto River, where Santa Anna was waiting for reinforcements. As the two armies lay in sight of one another at 9 A.M. on April 20, General Martin Perfecto de Cos arrived with 540 more soldiers to boost Santa Anna's advantage to 1,500 against just 783 Texans.

As the day wore on, neither side made a move. But at 3:30 P.M. Houston, with no advance warning, mounted Saracen and ordered his men to attack in two long skirmish lines. Catching the Mexicans off guard while they were resting, the Texans advanced to within forty yards before being spotted.

Then, shrieking "Remember the Alamo!" and "Remember Goliad!", they charged wildly into the enemy camp led by Houston on Saracen, who was hit by one of the first Mexican volleys. Houston jumped off his wounded horse and mounted another, only to have that horse shot from under him as well. Houston was also hit by a musket ball that ripped through his boot, shattering two bones in his leg and causing severe blood loss and excruciating pain.

After maneuvering Santa Anna into a poor military position and striking at the most opportune time, Houston scored a brilliant victory in a battle that lasted only minutes. In his official report to Burnet dated April 25, Houston wrote:

> The conflict lasted about eighteen minutes from the time of close action until we were in possession of the enemy's encampment. Our cavalry had charged and routed that of the enemy upon the right and given pursuit to the fugitives, which did not cease until they arrived at the bridge which I have mentioned. The conflict in the breastworks lasted but a few moments. Many of the troops [fought] hand to hand, and not having the advantage of bayonets on our side, our riflemen used their pieces as war clubs, breaking many of them off at the breech. [63]

By nightfall Houston's men had killed 630 Mexican soldiers, wounded 208, and captured 730 prisoners; only 6 Texans were killed (2 more would die a few days later) and 24 wounded. It was one of the

*In the Battle of San Jacinto, Texans led by Sam Houston triumphed in just
a few minutes, achieving one of the most legendary victories in U.S. history.*

greatest military victories in U.S. history
but Burnet, jealous of the glory Houston
won in the famous battle, would later
complain "he did not make the battle, but
the battle made him."[64]

THE REPUBLIC OF TEXAS

Texas soldiers hungry to avenge those
killed at the Alamo and Goliad were mer-
ciless in slaying the routed Mexicans. But
when Santa Anna was captured the next
day hiding in a swamp, wearing the
clothes of an ordinary soldier as a dis-
guise, Houston treated him respectfully
because he wanted to make peace with

Mexico. On May 14 Texas signed a treaty
with Santa Anna that ended the war and
extended the new republic's boundaries
to the Rio Grande, 150 miles further south
and west than the Nueces River, the original border of the Mexican province.

The treaty was disputed by the Mexican Congress, the only body legally
empowered to approve the agreement,
but Texas had won its freedom even if
Mexico failed to acknowledge the fact. Its
new borders encompassed today's state of
Texas as well as parts of present-day New
Mexico, Colorado, Wyoming, Kansas, and
Oklahoma. (In 1850 Texas would sell that
territory to the United States for $10 mil-
lion.)

TEXAS VENGEANCE

In war, the blood lust of battle and the hatred soldiers learn to feel for the enemy can lead to acts of great brutality. When General Santa Anna raised the black flag of "no quarter" at the Alamo and Goliad, his troops were ordered to kill defenseless men. When Sam Houston's men surprised and overwhelmed sleeping Mexican soldiers at San Jacinto, they also showed no mercy.

In his biography of Sam Houston, John Hoyt Williams describes how Texian soldiers killed Mexicans during the battle and kept on slaying them after victory had been secured.

"The Mexicans, raked with grapeshot, horseshoes and musketry, fell in heaps; some dropped their weapons in panic and fled to the rear. Mexicans fought screaming Texians, flailing away in hand-to-hand combat, until [as John Swisher said] 'their brains were dashed out with clubbed guns. '

Within minutes of the first Texian volley, most of the Mexican line was crushed and the rest in flight. Screeching 'Remember the Alamo' and 'Remember Goliad,' the Texians on this occasion fought under a figurative black flag, dispatching Mexicans, armed or unarmed, with bullet, gunstock, knife, and tomahawk. The slaughter was appalling. Cornered Mexicans fell to their knees in a largely vain attempt to save their lives, shouting, 'Me no Alamo.'

Hundreds of Mexicans fled mindlessly into the [San Jacinto] river, the swamp or the lagoon behind their camp. There, most died by drowning or bullet. As Robert Hancock Hunter clinically observed, 'that lagune was full of men & horses for about 20 feet or more up & down it, & non of them ever got out. I think there bones are laying there yet.' Hunter, who later guarded Santa Anna, recalled that 'Santa Anna said that it was not a Battle, that he cald it a massacre.'"

On September 5, 1836, voters elected Houston president by an overwhelming margin: 5,199 to only 745 for Henry Smith and 587 for Austin, the "Father of Texas" who had brought in the first settlers. "We now occupy the proud title of a sovereign and independent nation," proclaimed Houston, "which will impose on us the obligation of [showing] the world that we are worthy to be free." [65]

However, residents of the new Lone Star Republic—the nickname came from the single star on its flag, which also graced its currency, called "Star" bills— were eager to give up that sovereignty; in a referendum in the election, only ninety-two people voted against seeking annexation of Texas by the United States. However, it would be nine years before that would occur. And annexation, the legal process in which America welcomed Texas into the Union as its twenty-eighth state in 1845, would trigger war with Mexico.

THE MORMON MIGRATION

The present-day state of Utah was originally established by the Mormons as Deseret, a word from the sacred Book of Mormon meaning "honeybee." The Mormons were members of the Church of Jesus Christ of Latter-day Saints, which was founded by Joseph Smith on June 6, 1830, near Rochester, New York.

A farmer's son, Smith claimed he was visited in 1827 by the angel Moroni, who revealed the location of a sacred book—the Book of Mormon—written on golden tablets and buried in western New York near Palmyra. According to Smith, he unearthed the book from its secret hiding place. He published it in 1830, asserting it contained missing parts of the Bible, including accounts that Jesus Christ visited the New World after his crucifixion in Jerusalem. He also said the angel Moroni instructed him to found a new, true Christian church based on the book.

When Smith's church began to grow in upper New York State, he and his followers, who were called both Mormons and Saints, were persecuted by other Christians who considered their beliefs heresy. Hostility directed against the Mormons

Nauvoo, Illinois, was a refuge to Mormons before they had to flee from religious persecution.

forced them to move to Kirtland, Ohio, and then to Missouri, where they were so hated that Governor Lilburn Boggs in 1838 decreed "Mormons must be treated as enemies and must be exterminated or driven from the state, if necessary, for the public good."[66]

After mobs violently attacked the Mormons, killing nineteen of them and destroying much of their property, about fifteen thousand escaped to Illinois. On the banks of the Mississippi River, the Mormons built Nauvoo, which quickly became the frontier state's largest, most prosperous city; its name stemmed from the Hebrew word *nawa*, meaning "beautiful place." Illinois residents left Mormons in peace until Smith received another revelation from God, one that said high-ranking Mormons had the right to take multiple wives, a practice called polygamy.

When Illinois residents began turning against the Mormons in the belief that polygamy was illegal and immoral, Smith decided his followers needed to move far away from other people for their own safety. In a diary entry dated February 20, 1844, Smith wrote that the Mormons would seek a homeland in the far west:

> I instructed the Twelve Apostles to send out a delegation, and hunt out a good location where we can remove to, build a city in a day, and have a government of our own, get up into the mountains, where the devil cannot dig us out, and live in a healthy climate where we can live as old as we have a mind to.[67]

It was a bold move because the Great Plains between the settled east and the Pacific Coast were largely unknown, with much of it still held by Mexico. But like the Pilgrims who fled religious persecution in England to settle in the New World, the Mormons felt they had no choice but to brave the wilderness. Unfortunately, Smith did not act in time to save himself.

Within a few months the Mormon leader was arrested and jailed in Carthage, Illinois, on charges that he ordered the destruction of a printing press by a dissident Mormon group that opposed polygamy. "I am going like a lamb to the slaughter," Smith said when he was arrested, "but I am calm as a summer morning."[68] The Mormon leader's comment was prophetic. On June 27, 1844, an anti-Mormon mob of two hundred broke into the jail and shot to death Smith and his brother, Hyrum.

Brigham Young, the new Mormon leader, took up Smith's plan to find a refuge in the West and commanded everyone who was a member of the church to move there. The Mormons began their trek toward their new home February 4, 1846. By the end of the year Nauvoo was a ghost town, and some fifteen thousand Mormons traveling in three thousand wagons had pushed across Iowa to the banks of the Missouri River, where they rested for the winter.

The Mormons followed the Oregon Trail, a route established by pioneers migrating to Oregon Country, but at South Pass the Mormons headed southwest instead of north. On July 22, 1847, the first group of Mormons reached the valley of

MORMON GOVERNMENT

When the Mormons began to make their home in what would become Utah, Brigham Young devised a new system of government which was based on religion as well as democracy. In The Far Western Fronter: 1830-1860, *author Ray Allen Billington describes this form of government:*

"There was little room for popular rule in this system. No [Mormon] could think of voting against a candidate selected by God through Brigham Young. This gave the president absolute control over every subordinate down to the lowest ward bishop; the Mormon system was not a democracy but an oligarchy, 'working under and deadening the forms of democracy,' as one traveler put it. This to the Saints was the ideal government. By delegating to Young complete control over their affairs, spiritual and temporal alike, they assured themselves the guidance of Divine will which he alone understood. No problem could be solved, no decision made, without 'asking counsel' of this infinitely wise man.

Nor was his judgment ever questioned, whether he was ordering one of his followers into a distant mission field or proclaiming a new religious doctrine. More remarkable was the fact that passing Gentiles found the Mormon government system so just they frequently submitted their own disputes to its courts for settlement, always with satisfaction."

Brigham Young in a photograph taken many years after he led Mormons to their new home in what today is Utah.

the Great Salt Lake, where they decided to make their home in an area the United States would soon win in its war with Mexico. Mormon legend claims that when Young, ill with mountain fever, first saw the valley, he rose from his sickbed and proclaimed, "This is the place."[69]

By that fall about one thousand men, women, and children had arrived. For years Mormons continued to pour into the area from eastern states as well as from many European countries, where the Mormons recruited new settlers who were willing to accept their faith. On March 12, 1849, the Mormons ratified a constitution that was a blend of religion and democracy. Young was elected governor and the other officials were all Mormons, even though some non-Mormons had moved to Deseret—whose borders the Mormons claimed stretched from the Rockies to the Sierras and on to the Pacific Ocean in southern California.

Because Young and other church officials held supreme power over the lives of faithful believers, they were able to create a much more orderly settlement than those in many other frontier areas. Deseret soon became a thriving far west outpost. By 1860 it had sixty thousand residents. When a young journalist named Samuel Clemens visited there in 1863, he was surprised at the Mormons' unique lifestyle. Clemens, who would become world famous under his pen name, Mark Twain, wrote:

> I enjoyed the pleasant strangeness of a city of fifteen thousand inhabitants with no loafers perceptible in it; and no visible drunkards or noisy people; a limpid stream rippling and dancing through every street in place of a filthy gutter; block after block of trim dwellings, built of "frame" and sunburned brick; a grand general air of neatness, repair, thrift, and comfort, around and about the whole. And everywhere were workshops, factories, and all manners of industries; and intent faces and busy hands were to be seen wherever one looked; and in one's ears was the ceaseless clink of the hammers, the buzz of trade and the contented hum of drums and flywheels. [70]

Like the Texans before them, the Mormons sought statehood. But their first bid to join the Union in 1849 was rejected, as were five subsequent attempts between 1856 and 1887. The area was finally admitted into the Union in 1896 after Mormon leaders agreed to discontinue polygamy and allow non-Mormons to participate in governing the new state, which was called Utah.

Both Texans and the Mormons had carved new nations out of the wilderness. But the fate of Deseret and Texas, was to be consumed by a political philosophy that captured the imagination of Americans—Manifest Destiny.

4 Manifest Destiny: License to Conquer

In 1837 when the United States was considering annexing Texas, William Ellery Channing, a Unitarian leader and pioneering pacifist, was one of the voices raised against bringing the Lone Star Republic into the Union:

> Possessed of a domain, vast enough for the growth of ages, it is time for us to stop in the career of acquisition and conquest. Our Eagle will whet, not gorge its appetite on its first victim; and will [scent] a more tempting quarry, more alluring blood in every new region which opens southward. To annex Texas is to declare perpetual war with Mexico. [71]

Channing and many others believed the United States was already big enough. When America won its freedom in the Revolutionary War, it was already four times larger (860,000 square miles) than France, Europe's largest nation, and the Louisiana Purchase made it bigger than all of Europe with the exception of the gigantic Russian empire.

But in 1845 the United States did annex Texas and, as Channing predicted, went to war with Mexico. As Channing also foresaw, the acquisition only made the United States hungrier for more land, with the result that it would bully Great Britain out of the Oregon Country and also seize the Mexican provinces of California and New Mexico.

This was all done in the spirit of Manifest Destiny, a term coined in an 1845 editorial by John L. O'Sullivan in New York's *Democratic Review*. "It is our Manifest Destiny," he wrote, "to overspread the continent allotted by Providence for the free development of our yearly multiplying millions."[72] For many, Manifest Destiny was a crusade not only to add new land but, as stated by future president James Buchanan, "to extend the blessing of Christianity and religious liberty over the whole continent."[73]

It was a philosophy that made Americans believe they had the God-given right to seize whatever land they were strong enough to hold. And in 1846 they did, starting with the Oregon Country, the first area to lure settlers across an entire continent.

OREGON COUNTRY

In 1792 New England ship captain Robert Gray provided the first American claim to

Manifest Destiny and Racism

The most troubling underlying rationale of Manifest Destiny was a persistent, widespread racism that led Americans to consider nonwhite people inferior. Missouri Senator Thomas Hart Benton commented on the racial aspects of Manifest Destiny in a speech given on May 28, 1846, quoted in Distant Horizon: Documents from the Nineteenth-Century American West.

"The Mongolian or Yellow race is far above the Ethiopian, or Black, and above the American Indian, or Red; it is a race far above these, but still, far below the White; and like all the rest, must receive an impression from the superior race whenever they come in contact. It would seem that the white race alone received the divine command to subdue, and replenish the earth! For it is the only race that has obeyed it—the only one that hunts out new and distant lands, and even a New World, to subdue and replenish.

I cannot murmur at what seems to be the effect of divine law. I cannot repent that this Capital [Washington, D.C.] has replaced the wigwam—this Christian people replaced the savages—white matrons the red squaws. Civilization, or extinction, has been the fate of all people who have found themselves in the track of the advancing Whites, and civilization, always the preference of the Whites, has been pressed as an object, while extinction has followed as the consequences of its resistance."

the region by locating the place where the Columbia River emptied into the Pacific Ocean. In 1805 the arrival of the Lewis and Clark expedition on the Pacific Coast strengthened America's rights to Oregon Country, an area that included present-day Oregon as well as Washington, Idaho, and part of Montana.

Spain and Russia were also engaged in the fur trade in the Oregon Country in the 1700s, but gradually withdrew from the area, leaving Great Britain and the United States to vie for control. In 1818 the two remaining competitors agreed to joint occupation, an uneasy truce that existed for nearly three decades as they both sought to strengthen their presence in hopes of ousting the other nation.

It was not until Boston businessman Nathaniel Wyeth ventured to Oregon Country in 1832 and brought home favorable reports of the lush Willamette Valley that Americans began to consider the Northwest for settlement. The first to move there were missionaries inspired by four Indians—three Flathead and a Nez Percé—who journeyed to St. Louis. A letter in the March 1, 1833, issue of the

Methodist *Christian Advocate and Journal* claiming the Indians traveled across a continent from Oregon Country to learn about the white man's "book of Heaven" touched off an ecclesiastical crusade to save the souls of Native Americans. Writes historian Sanford Wexler:

> Almost overnight every religious person in the United States became concerned with the plight of the Indians who had traveled 2,000 miles to hear the word of God. One single letter did more to stimulate interest in the Oregon Country than all the efforts of Wyeth [and others], and the pleas to Congress by politicians and explorers. [74]

Several Methodist missionaries traveled to to the Willamette Valley in 1834, and two years later Dr. Marcus Whitman, a Presbyterian, arrived from western New York with his wife, Narcissa, to establish missions for the Cayuse, Nez Percé, and Flathead tribes. They made the rugged journey over the Oregon Trail, a two thousand-mile route that started in Independence, Missouri. The trail followed the Platte River until it forked, and then proceeded along the North Platte to South Pass, the only passage through the Rocky Mountains; on the other side it dropped south to Fort Bridger and then ran northwesterly along several rivers to Oregon. By heading in a different direction once they went through South Pass, later travelers

A wagon train plods slowly west across the vast frontier. The rugged, dangerous journey lasted months.

were able to use this route to get to California and Utah.

Death from illness, accident, and confrontations with Indians was a common occurrence along the Oregon Trail. It is estimated that during the years the trail was used, at least seventeen people died for every mile. Francis Parkman, who traveled the Oregon Trail in 1846 and wrote a book that helped make it famous, describes finding grave markers that pioneers put up for loved ones who died:

> Some times we passed the grave of one who had sickened and died on the way. One morning, a piece of plank, standing upright on the summit of a grassy hill, attracted our notice, and riding up to it, we found the following words very thoroughly traced upon it, apparently with a red-hot piece of iron:
>
> MARY ELLIS
>
> Died May 7th, 1845
>
> aged two months. [75]

For those who traveled the Oregon Trail, the phrase, "Have you seen the elephant?"[76] was a shorthand query symbolizing the danger, excitement, and hardship they encountered during their long, difficult journeys. In this era, hardly any American had ever seen an elephant; the aura of mystery surrounding this little-known, exotic animal represented the many strange things pioneers saw and the adventures they experienced as they headed west.

In 1840 there were only about one hundred Americans in Oregon Country, but in 1843 some fifteen hundred hardy souls were the first of several thousand who would journey there in what came to be called "The Great Migration." They ventured to a far-off frontier because of glowing reports such as this exaggerated praise from one visitor, who declared Oregon Country "a pioneer's paradise" where "the pigs are already cooked, with knives and forks sticking in them so that you can cut off a slice if you are hungry."[77]

So many people migrated to Oregon Country in the early 1840s that President James K. Polk commented in his March 4, 1845, inaugural speech that "our title to the Country of Oregon is clear and unquestionable, and already our people are [securing] that title by occupying it with their wives and children." [78]

He was correct. "Oregon fever" had infected so many in the East that by 1846 Americans outnumbered the British in Oregon five thousand to only seven hundred; it was only a matter of time before the United States would seize the area.

PRESIDENT POLK: EXPANSIONIST

The growing number of Americans living in Oregon Country strengthened the resolve of the nation to claim it exclusively. But the increasingly loud cry by citizens to take Oregon was just one facet of the growing strength of Manifest Destiny, which in the mid-1840s had Americans casting acquisitive glances on new territory all the way west to the Pacific Ocean.

The 1844 presidential election had been decided on two issues relating to Westward

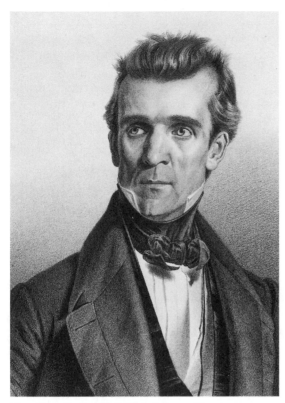

President James K. Polk led the nation to war against Mexico and forced Great Britain to give up its claim to the Oregon Country.

Expansion: annexation of Texas and U.S. ownership of the Oregon Country. A forceful stand on those issues helped Polk, a Democrat, defeat Whig candidate Henry Clay; many of the votes came from residents of western states, who had already benefited from the nation's continued growth. Historian Thomas Bailey writes that the election signaled a new era of government-backed Westward Expansion:

> The campaign of 1844 was in part an expression of the mighty emotional upsurge known as Manifest Destiny. Countless citizens in the 1840s and 1850s, feeling a sense of mission, believed that Almighty God had "manifestly" destined the American people [to] irresistibly spread their uplifting and ennobling democratic institutions over at least the entire continent. Land greed and ideals were thus co-joined.[79]

Although Polk vowed he would waste no time in fulfilling his campaign promises once he succeeded President John Tyler, the outgoing president acted first on the issue of Texas.

By 1845 the Lone Star Republic had been in existence for nine years. Although its population had grown, Texas was struggling financially, and its future was precarious because Mexico had never formally recognized its independence and continued to pose a military threat. With Polk's support, Tyler pushed through Congress a joint resolution annexing Texas, signing the measure March 1, 1845, just three days before Polk became president. By the end of the year, Texas would become the nation's twenty-eighth state.

Once he was president, Polk moved speedily on the Oregon issue. Just a few months after taking office, Polk told the British that joint occupation of the disputed territory must end, and he began talks to formalize a U.S. takeover of the area. Missouri Senator Thomas Hart Benton, one of the most forceful advocates of expansion, echoed public sentiment when he said he did not fear war with Britain: "Let the emigrants go on [to Oregon] and carry rifles. They will make all quiet there."[80]

Jesse A. Applegate : Oregon Pioneer

In 1843, one of those making the "Great Migration" to Oregon Country was Jesse A. Applegate, a young man from Missouri. Applegate later wrote a book about the six-month cross-country trek and his family's hard work to build a new home in the Willamette Valley in Oregon.

These excerpts from his book are from In Their Own Words: Warriors and Pioneers.

[Applegate notes the joy of reaching Oregon.] "A train of wagons with their once white, now torn, grease- and dust-stained covers, parked on the bank of the Columbia River was a novel spectacle. The faithful oxen, now sore-necked, sore-footed, and jaded, which had marched week after week, month after month drawing those wagons with their loads from the Missouri River to the Columbia, had done their task and were unhitched for the last time.

Father built his first cabin on the point of a ridge a hundred and fifty feet above the valley. He said that in the river bottoms where we lived in Missouri we had chills and fever. He wanted to build where we could get plenty of fresh air. In this he was not disappointed for the sea breeze kept the boards on the roof rattling all through the autumn season, and the first storm of winter blew the roof off.

In the course of three or four years after we began life in the wilderness of Salt Creek, we had pasture fenced, grain fields and gardens, small apple and peach orchards grown and quite a number of cattle, horses, hogs, and chickens. We had eatables in abundance."

The warlike words, however, were unnecessary. The two nations had jointly occupied the area since 1818 as far north as parallel 54°40′, a geographical boundary that during the 1844 campaign inspired the motto "fifty-four–forty or fight" by those who wanted Oregon Country as a U.S. possession. Polk had taken up that political chant himself, but once elected he was willing to compromise for two reasons: first, few Americans in Oregon Country lived that far north, almost all had settled below the 49th parallel; and second, because war with Mexico seemed inevitable, he did not want to risk fighting Great Britain at the same time.

On July 12 Secretary of State James Buchanan, who in 1856 would himself be elected president, told British officials the United States was willing to divide

Oregon Country along the 49th parallel. The British countered by demanding that the new boundary between the United States and Canada be the Columbia River, which was even further south than the 49th parallel. Negotiations continued into 1846, when the British realized it was not worth fighting over and agreed to the 49th parallel as a boundary line between the United States and Canada. The Senate ratified the Oregon Treaty on June 18, 1846, increasing the nation's size yet again.

WAR WITH MEXICO

When Polk had praised annexation of Texas in his inaugural speech, he enraged Mexico's minister to the United States, Juan Almonte. Almonte labeled the takeover of the former Mexican province "the most unjust aggression in the annals of modern history."[81] Before the end of March, Almonte would sever diplomatic relations with America and return to his homeland.

In an attempt to resolve the matter peacefully, in September 1845 Polk ordered John Slidell to go to Mexico City and offer $30 million to settle a dispute over the border between Texas and Mexico that had existed since Texas won its independence, satisfy U.S. claims against Mexico, and purchase New Mexico and California. When Mexico refused to meet with Slidell, the offended emissary angrily wrote Polk: "Depend upon it, we can never get along well with them, until we have given them a good drubbing." [82]

Slidell's tough talk stemmed from the fact that the United States did not fear Mexico militarily. The two nations had been engaged in trade since 1821, when William Becknell began hauling merchandise from Missouri to Santa Fe, the provincial capital of New Mexico. Historian Ray Allen Billington claims the Santa Fe trade created a sense of American contempt for Mexico:

> For two decades great caravans of wagons, laden with goods of every description, regularly plied the thousand-mile long trail between Missouri and New Mexico, bringing back good profits to enterprising merchants and revealing to all the United States the weakness of Mexico's hold upon its northern provinces. The trails blazed by the traders were soon to be followed by conquering armies.[83]

In a show of force to make Mexico more conciliatory, on January 12, 1846, Polk ordered General Zachary Taylor to Texas. Taylor arrived March 28 with a force of about four thousand soldiers and established a base in the disputed territory between the Nueces River and the Rio Grande. When Texas became a republic in 1836, it had claimed the Rio Grande as its southern boundary even though Mexico maintained the border should be the Nueces, which was 130 miles further north.

Mexican dictator Santa Anna countered by dispatching fifty-seven hundred troops to Matamoros, a small town opposite the U.S. encampment. The two sides had several minor skirmishes, and the flashpoint came on April 25, when a

Shown mounted on a white horse, General Zachary Taylor led U.S. troops to a series of victories in northern Mexico.

reconnoitering party of sixty-three U.S. soldiers was attacked on the north side of the Rio Grande by sixteen hundred Mexican cavalry. Eleven Americans died, five were wounded, and the rest captured in an incident that triggered war.

After hearing of the attack on U.S. forces, Polk on May 11, 1846, told Congress:

> Mexico has passed the boundary of the United States, has invaded our territory and shed American blood upon American soil. She has proclaimed that hostilities have commenced, and that the two nations are now at war. As war exists, and, notwithstanding all our efforts to avoid it, exists by the act of Mexico

herself . . . I invoke the prompt action of Congress [to declare war].[84]

Congress quickly agreed and on May 13 Polk signed the war declaration.

NOT JUST TEXAS WAS AT STAKE

Although Polk claimed Mexico started the war, it was really only reacting to Polk's occupation of the disputed territory, which Mexico considered an insult. Once American forces were deployed there, war was inevitable, and most historians believe Polk issued the order because he wanted a war not only to settle the Texas question but also as an excuse to seize other Mexican territory. Writes historian Harold Faber:

> The vision of Golden California as part of the United States was the real cause of the Mexican War. There were tensions on the Mexican border, there were problems concerning the annexation of Texas, there were insults and misunderstandings on both sides. But behind the hostile attitudes and moves was the fact that the United States was determined to expand to the Pacific. Neither Indians nor the elements nor the legality of Mexican claims was going to stand in the way. [85]

In addition to Native American tribes that had been subjugated by the Spanish, California in 1846 was lightly populated by Mexican citizens and about eight hundred Americans. But Polk and other officials saw tremendous potential in its mild climate and long Pacific coast, which would give the nation ports for its growing Far East trade. New Mexico, a mostly desert region, was also deemed valuable because of the lucrative Santa Fe trade. So, the Mexican War was fought over much more than just Texas.

WINNING THE WAR

In *The Shaping of the American Past*, Robert Kelley writes that "for the Mexicans, the war was a disaster from beginning to end."[86] Although Mexico's army was larger, Americans had more accurate weapons, better military leaders, and more funds to conduct war than its impoverished foe.

Taylor's army of six thousand invaded northern Mexico while a smaller force of about fifteen hundred under Colonel Stephen W. Kearny was sent to occupy New Mexico and California. Kearny encountered little resistance in either Mexican province, with both falling into American hands by August. On August 19, a day after capturing Santa Fe, Kearny tried to reassure frightened Mexican citizens that they would not be harmed: "New Mexicans! We have come amongst you to take possession of New Mexico, which we do in the name of the United States. We have come with peaceable intentions and kind feelings toward you all. We do not mean to murder you or rob you of your property." [87]

Taylor's army, meanwhile, was forcing its way south into Mexico in a series of military victories that began with the Battle of Palo Alto May 8, an engagement that was fought and won five days before the United States officially declared war. Although Taylor had many triumphs, including the seizure of Yerba Buena on July 9 and his defeat of a major Mexican force at the Battle of Buena Vista in February 1847, he never advanced far enough south to win the war.

In 1847, Polk sent General Winfield Scott with a second army of ten thousand by sea from New Orleans to Vera Cruz, where the Americans landed and captured the port city. Marching inland with a force increased to fourteen thousand by the arrival of more soldiers, Scott captured Mexico City on September 14, 1847, in the war's final military action.

General Winfield Scott directs his soldiers in the battle for Vera Cruz.

One of the heroes of the concluding battle was Second Lieutenant Ulysses S. Grant, who would later lead Union forces in the Civil War and go on to be elected president. In the battle to capture Chapultepec Hill, a key defensive position west of Mexico City, Grant commandeered space in a church tower for a better position to attack opposing soldiers with a small cannon. Grant explains how this occurred:

> I found a church, which looked to me as if the belfry would command the [field of fire]. . . . When I knocked for admission a priest came to the door, who, while extremely polite, declined to admit us. With the little Spanish at my command, I explained to him he might save property by opening the

door, and he certainly would save himself from becoming a prisoner. . . . He began to see his duty in the same light that I did, and opened the door. . . . The shots from our little gun dropped in upon the enemy and created great confusion. [88]

Grant's heroics helped U.S. forces capture Mexico City and end the war. On September 18, 1847, Scott boasted of his victory in a dispatch: "At the end of another series of arduous and brilliant operations, this glorious army hoisted, on the morning of the 14th, the colors of the United States on the walls [of the National Palace of Mexico]." [89]

Defeated on all fronts, Mexico had no choice but to negotiate peace terms to end the war. In the Treaty of Guadalupe Hidalgo, signed February 2, 1848, the United States gave Mexico $15 million as well as an additional $3.5 million to settle claims against Mexico by U.S. citizens. In return, the United States received all or part of what today are the states of New Mexico, Utah, Nevada, Arizona, California, Texas, Colorado, and Wyoming. The cost of victory, however, was much higher than that small sum—the bill to wage the war was $100 million and, on a human level, thirteen thousand U.S. soldiers lost their lives.

Historian John Hawgood claims the more than five hundred thousand square miles of land America won "ranks in importance with the Louisiana Purchase in the history of the American west. It gave to the United States her empire on the Pacific, for which she had so long striven." [90]

WOMEN ON THE TRAIL

Life on the Oregon Trail was hard on everyone but especially so for women, who had to do everything from fixing breakfast to fixing wagons. The authors of Nation of Nations: A Narrative History of the American Republic *claim "the journey west placed a special strain on women," who assumed duties they never had to handle before while still performing traditional feminine tasks of cooking and cleaning.*

"Necessity placed new demands on women and eventually altered their roles. At first, parties divided work by gender, as had been done back home. Women cooked, washed, sewed, and took care of the children, while men drove the wagons, cared for the stock, stood guard, and did the heavy labor. Within a few weeks, however, women found themselves engaged in the distinctly unladylike task of gathering buffalo dung for fuel on the treeless plains or pitching in to help repair wagons or construct a bridge. When men became exhausted, sick, or injured, women stood guard and drove the oxen.

The change in work assignments proceeded only in one direction, however, for few men undertook 'women's work' and no matter how late the previous night's chores had continued, women had to be up before daybreak, ahead of the men, preparing the next morning's meal.

The extra labor did not bring women new authority or power within the family. [However] one woman reports that there was 'not a little fighting' in their company, which was 'invariably the outcome of disputes over divisions of labor.'"

FREE OR SLAVE?

After the victory over Mexico the issue of slavery, which Thomas Jefferson once called "a fire bell in the night,"[91] began to sound its ugly refrain across the land. When Congress approved annexation of Texas, it stipulated the new area would yield four new states. With Oregon, Cal-ifornia, New Mexico, and Utah also pre-paring to join the Union, the uneasy bal-ance that had existed for decades between northern states, which had outlawed slav-ery, and southern slave states, reached a crisis.

Texas, which had refused Mexico's de-mands to end slavery when it was still just a province of that nation, would be-

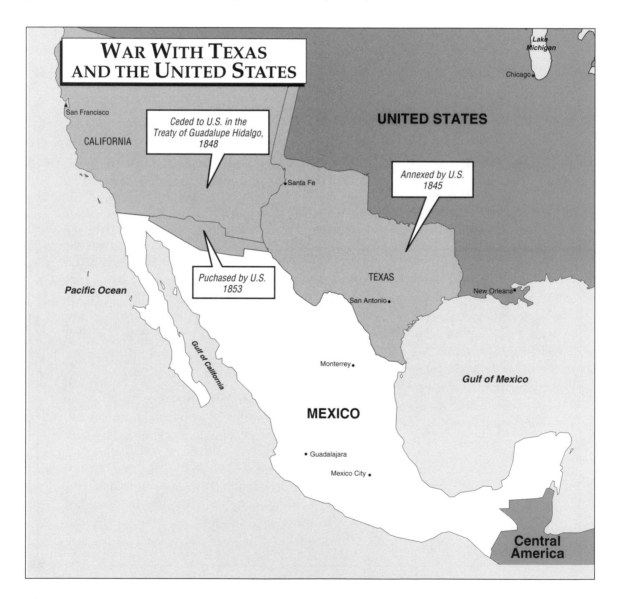

WAR WITH TEXAS AND THE UNITED STATES

Lake Michigan

Chicago

San Francisco

UNITED STATES

CALIFORNIA

Ceded to U.S. in the Treaty of Guadalupe Hidalgo, 1848

Santa Fe

Annexed by U.S. 1845

Purchased by U.S. 1853

TEXAS

Pacific Ocean

San Antonio

New Orleans

Gulf of California

Monterrey

Gulf of Mexico

MEXICO

Guadalajara

Mexico City

Central America

Kentucky Senator Henry Clay, architect of the Compromise of 1850.

After months of bitter debate, both sides agreed to a series of compromises offered by Senator Henry Clay of Kentucky. The complex proposal called for admitting California as a free state while allowing citizens in New Mexico and Utah to decide the issue themselves, creating a stronger law for the return of runaway slaves, and prohibiting the slave trade in the District of Columbia. The compromise measures were approved in 1850, clearing the way for orderly expansion while preserving the Union itself; some southern states had threatened to secede even then over the issue.

The situation was so tense that when the Compromise of 1850 was announced, people ran through the streets of Washington crying, "The Union is saved!" Senator Daniel Webster proclaimed:

> I can now sleep of nights. We have now gone through the most important crisis that has occurred since the foundation of this government, and whatever party may prevail, hereafter, the Union stands firm. Disunion, and the love of mischief, are put under, at least for the present, and I hope for a long time. [92]

But the Union Webster so loved would soon be pulled apart anyway by the issue of slavery.

come a slave state, but what about the others? The issue came to a head on December 3, 1849, when the California Territory asked to be admitted to the Union with a constitution prohibiting slavery. Southerners were outraged that slavery would be denied settlers in California and tried to block statehood. The issue of slavery, which in little more than a decade would lead north and south into civil war, was even now slowing the Westward Expansion.

5 Gold in California Sparks a New Wave of Settlement

The May 29, 1848, edition of the San Francisco *Californian* carried this news story:

> The whole country, from San Francisco to Los Angeles and from the sea shore to the base of the Sierra Nevada, resounds with the sordid cry of "*gold*!! **GOLD!!!**" while the field is left half planted, the house half built, and everything neglected but the manufacturers of shovels and pickaxes, and the means of transportation to the spot where one man obtained $128 worth of the *real stuff* in one day's washing. [93]

On January 24 James Marshall discovered gold while building a sawmill on the American River for Johann Augustus Sutter, a Swiss immigrant who in 1839 had persuaded Mexico to grant him a huge tract of land on the Sacramento River. At the Sacramento's junction with the American River, Sutter established the colony of Nueva Helvetia (New Switzerland), also called Sutter's Fort, which later became the city of Sacramento.

Coming only a week before the treaty with Mexico made California a U.S. possession, the discovery galvanized the nation and sparked a massive influx of gold seekers from throughout America and around the world. By early 1849 nearly five thousand had raced to the gold fields and by the end of the year between forty thou-

Johann Augustus Sutter, on whose land gold was discovered, touching off a mad dash for riches.

MORMON HANDCARTS

By 1855 so many people were immigrating from Europe to join the Mormons that the religious group ran low on funds to transport them to the new homeland it was creating in Utah. Brigham Young suggested a novel way for newcomers to make the journey across the Great Plains—by handcart—because the carts were cheaper to make than large wagons. In The Far Western Frontier: 1830–1860, *author Ray Allen Billington explains this unique experiment in transportation:*

"Why not, [Young] reasoned, substitute handcarts for expensive covered wagons? Pushing these, immigrants could average fifteen miles daily, crossing the plains in seventy days. That autumn Mormon carpenters in Iowa began building carts, which were waiting by the hundreds when new arrivals began flocking in during the spring of 1856. On June 9 and June 11 the first two companies of 947 persons, with one hundred handcarts, went rolling out of Iowa City, singing as they trudged along:

Who cares to go with the wagons?

Not we who are free and strong;

Our faith and arms, with right good will,

Shall pull our carts along."

By September 26, 1856, they were in Salt Lake City, "somewhat fatigued," but still buoyant and cheerful, having outdistanced every wagon train on the trail. A third party arrived safely on October 2. But when the other two handcart brigades left late, they were caught in early winter snows in the Rocky Mountains. Of the 1,000 people in the two parties, 225 perished in one of the major disasters of overland travel during the nation's Westward Expansion.

sand and fifty thousand "Forty-Niners," as they were called, had arrived to stake their claims.

The lust for metallic riches lured a new breed of pioneer westward. Instead of families in search of fertile farmland, the newcomers who swarmed the gold fields were nearly all male and included adventurers, gamblers, and petty criminals, along with 40 percent of the enlisted men serving in California, who deserted the U.S. Army to seek their fortunes. The following chorus from a song popular during the gold rush jokes about the type of men who migrated to California:

Oh what was your name in the States?

Was it Thompson or Johnson or Bates?

Did you murder your wife; And fly for your Life?

Say, what was your name in the States? [94]

But gold hunters were only the vanguard of a new wave of settlers who flowed into the vast new lands won in the Mexican War as well as other frontier areas. Between the gold rush period and the Civil War, Americans also began filling up Texas, Utah, and the new states of Kansas and Nebraska. Fanny Kelly, one of the first settlers in the Kansas territory created in 1854, wrote about the streams of Americans crossing the Great Plains:

> The years 1852 to 1856 witnessed, probably, the heaviest immigration the West had ever known in a corresponding length of time. Those who had gone before sent back to their friends such marvelous accounts of the fertility of the soil, their rapid development of the country, and the ease with which fortunes were made, the "Western fever" became almost epidemic. Whole towns in the old, Eastern States were almost depopulated. Old substantial farmers, surrounded by all the comforts that the heart could wish, sacrificed the homes wherein their families had been reared for generations, and, with all their worldly pos-

sessions, turned their faces toward the setting sun. [95]

CALIFORNIA

The Spanish had settled California in 1769 when Father Junípero Serra led a small group of Franciscan missionaries into the little-known area. Spain established a string of twenty-one missions that became centers for farming and ranching as well as four presidios (forts) at San Diego, Santa Barbara, San Francisco, and Monterey, the capital, and by 1820 there were about three thousand Spanish residents, who were called Californios. In 1833 mission lands were broken up and individuals received huge tracts of land called ranchos for California's major industry, raising cattle for beef and hides.

The first American arrivals, trappers and sea traders, sent back glowing reports of a new land that one mountain man termed "a perfect paradise, a perpetual spring." [96] In 1841 a group of thirty-seven pioneers from the Missouri frontier led by John Bidwell were the first to move to California, settling down in the San Joaquin Valley, but by 1846 there were still only about five hundred Americans compared to eight thousand to twelve thousand Mexican citizens.

Although small in numbers, the Americans reacted daringly when news of war with Mexico reached California. On June 14, just a month after war had been declared, a small band of self-styled patriots captured the lightly guarded city of Sonoma and forced Mexican official Mariano G. Vallejo to surrender all of California. When army captain John Charles Frémont arrived at Sonoma on June 25 with a small detachment, he threw his support behind this informal Bear Flag Revolt, which took its name from a homemade white flag featuring a grizzly bear facing a red star.

Frémont was appointed military governor of the "Republic of California." But the fledgling nation survived only until July 9, when naval forces under Commodore John D. Sloat arrived to occupy San Francisco and Sonoma, claim California for the United States, and replace the bear flag with the American flag.

The son-in-law of Senator Thomas Hart

Captain John Frémont helped open the West by exploring, mapping, and writing about previously unknown parts of the Southwest and the Great Plains.

Benton, the arch-expansionist from Missouri, Frémont played a strange role during this tense period in California history. It is believed Frémont was sent there with sixty buckskin-clad frontiersmen not to explore and map the area, duties that had made him famous during several expeditions from 1839 to 1846, but to provide American might in case of war with Mexico. "Fremont's conduct," Sutter wrote, "was extremely mysterious. Flitting about the country with an armed body of men, he was regarded with suspicion by everybody." [97]

A year later Frémont was court-martialed for disobedience and sentenced to dismissal, but President James K. Polk, swayed by the powerful Benton, set aside the penalty. Frémont resigned from the military, became a multimillionaire in the gold fields, and in 1850 was elected one of the state's first senators. He ran unsuccessfully for president in 1856 as a Republican, losing to Democrat James Buchanan.

GOLD! GOLD! GOLD!

It took six months for word of the gold strike to reach eastern states, but when it did, the news created a sensation. Those with enough money ($368) boarded ships that sailed around Panama to California in six to eight weeks, while those less prosperous set out on the difficult overland journey of several months. In 1849 an estimated eighty thousand Forty-Niners traveled to California, most of them (fifty-five thousand) cross-country by horse or wagon.

JAMES MARSHALL DISCOVERS GOLD!

His task was to build a sawmill on the American River. Instead, James Marshall on that fateful day in 1848 discovered gold, opening the way for an exciting new era in the history of America's Westward Expansion. The following paragraphs taken from The Heritage of America *by Henry Steele Commager and Allan Nevins are part of Marshall's personal account of one of the key events that fueled Westward Expansion.*

"It was a clear cold morning [January 24, 1848]; I shall never forget that morning—as I was taking my usual walk along the millrace, after shutting off the water my eye was caught by a glimpse of something shining in the bottom of the ditch. There was about a foot of water running there, I reached my hand down and picked it up; it made my heart thump, for I felt certain it was gold. The piece was about half the size and of the shape of a pea. Then I saw another piece in the water.

After taking it out I sat down and began to think right hard. I thought it was gold and yet it did not seem to be of the right color; all the gold coin I had seen of was of a reddish tinge; this looked more like brass. When I returned to our cabin for breakfast I showed the two pieces to my men. They were all a good deal excited, and had they not thought that the gold only existed in small quantities they would have abandoned everything and left me to finish the job alone.

[Marshall told his employer, Johann Sutter, he had found gold.] This fact being ascertained, we thought it our

best policy to keep it as quiet as possible till we should have finished our mill, but [the news] just spread like wildfire and [would-be miners descended in hordes on Sutter's land.] Sometimes I had the greatest kind of trouble to get rid of them. I sent them all off in different directions, telling them about such and such places where I was certain there was plenty of gold if they would only take the trouble of looking for it."

James Marshall's discovery of gold ignited one of the most frantic periods of migration in the history of Westward Expansion.

One mining technique depended on water to wash away lighter dirt and debris, leaving the heavier gold behind. While one miner throws dirt into the running water, two others search for flakes and nuggets of gold.

They were lured west by fantastic accounts of how easy it was to find gold, such as this letter from the Reverend Walter Colton of Monterey that was printed in a Washington, D.C., newspaper on December 11, 1848: "At present the people are running over the country and picking gold out of the earth here and there, just as a thousand hogs let loose in a forest would root up the ground nuts." [98] In January 1849 New Yorker Philip Hone wrote in his diary about the madness that had swept the country: "Gold! Gold! The California fever is increasing in violence. Thousands are going, among whom are many young men of our best families." [99]

Men left their families to find a rich strike called a bonanza (Spanish for "fair weather"). One poorly educated prospec-tor wrote home from the gold fields: "Jane, i left you and them boys for no other reason than this to come here to procure a little property by the swet of my brow so that we could have a place of our own that i mite not be a dog for other people any long." [100]

By 1850 the estimated one hundred thousand new arrivals, 95 percent of them men, had helped California become the nation's thirty-first state. Women who followed found they could make their own fortunes by washing and cooking, skills most men did not have, or performing other jobs. One woman wrote a friend in the East, "A smart woman can do well in this country. It is the only country I ever was in where a woman received anything like a just compensation for work."[101] During this period, however, 20 percent of the women in California were employed as prostitutes.

After their long, arduous journeys, the thousands of prospective millionaires found crowded, primitive conditions in gold fields christened with colorful names such as Poker Flat, Whiskey Bark, Hell's Delight, and Skunk Gulch. Early arrivals with choice claims were able to gather three hundred to five hundred dollars a day in gold dust or nuggets, but the daily take kept going down as more miners arrived.

Although many Forty-Niners made small fortunes, they often spent their money as quickly as they earned it, either by wasting cash on good times in bars and gambling halls or simply living in mining camps where prices skyrocketed: eggs were ten dollars a dozen, month-old newspapers one dollar, and rooms up to one thousand dollars a month. Merchants who supplied miners often became wealthier than the prospectors; they were able to charge exorbitant prices because they had the only available supplies for miles around.

Among those venturing to the gold fields were an estimated two thousand free African Americans as well as many brought as slaves, some of whom mined enough gold to buy their freedom. When Daniel Rogers gave his Arkansas master a thousand dollars in gold dust, the slave holder refused to honor his agreement to free Rogers and demanded more. Other Arkansas whites were so upset at the treachery that they raised the additional money for Rogers and gave him a certificate praising his "honesty, industry and integrity." [102]

The influx of huge numbers of people and dazzling amounts of money led to explosive growth in cities like San Francisco, which from April to September of 1849 mushroomed from a small community with about forty homes and a few hundred residents to a thriving metropolis of five hundred houses and some six thousand people. Demand for housing was so high that carpenters in China and England built homes, took them apart in sections, and shipped them to the fabulously wealthy new city. In less than a decade Sutter's Fort grew into a major city, Sacramento, and other communities like Los Angeles sprang up quickly.

At the height of the boom in 1852 the state's population ballooned to 250,000, and miners that year extracted more than $81 million in gold from California rivers and soil. By 1855 the United States was producing almost half the world's gold.

EASTWARD EXPANSION

The discovery of gold touched off four decades of explosive Westward Expansion. But historian Richard Stiles writes that the get-rich-quick Forty-Niners and the tens of thousands of sturdy pioneers who followed created unbalanced national growth:

> Instead of a steady march of the frontier across the West, the gold rush led to a region weighted at both ends, on the coasts and in the Midwest, but

unsettled (by whites) from the Rocky Mountains to the Great Plains. The Great Plains in part emerged as a transit zone, a path for settlers and merchants bound for the Pacific. [103]

But when California gold production began to decline, prospectors who had failed to strike it rich began scouting other western areas. In 1858 gold was found sixty-five miles west of Pikes Peak in what is now Colorado, touching off another mad dash to new gold fields and another population boom. Within months hundreds of cabins and tents blossomed along Cherry Creek, and the city of Denver emerged. By 1861 Congress had separated Colorado from the Kansas Territory, and by 1865 Denver, with a population of five thousand, was known as the Queen City of the Plains.

The next big strike after Pikes Peak was the discovery in June 1859 of gold and silver in Nevada, which again lured miners by the thousands. The western Nevada mines were enormously rich and between 1859 and 1869 yielded $100 million in gold and silver—most of it from the fabulously wealthy Comstock Lode, which in 1867 alone produced $16.5 million in precious ore.

The constant search for new metallic wealth led to a strange phenomenon— eastward expansion into areas like present-day Colorado, Nevada, Arizona, Idaho, and Montana that had never previously been settled. *The Daily Oregonian* commented on this trend in its July 12, 1862, edition: "What a clover field is to a steer, the sky to the lark, a mudhole to a hog, such are newer diggings to a miner." [104]

In 1861 even a young journalist named Samuel Clemens, who had adopted the pen name Mark Twain, was lured from his job as a reporter for the *Virginia City (Nevada) Enterprise* to a new mining spot in Unionville, Nevada:

> I confess, without shame, that I expected to find masses of silver lying all about the ground. I expected to see it glittering in the sun on mountain summits. I was perfectly satisfied in my own mind as I could be of anything, that I was going to gather up, in a day or two, or at furthest a week or two, silver enough to make me satisfactorily wealthy—and so my fancy was already busy with plans for spending this money. [105]

Like most miners, Clemens never became rich. Many gold seekers who set out for Colorado in 1859 with banners proclaiming "Pikes Peak or Bust!" returned home empty-handed, their wagons bearing the unhappy new message "Busted, By God!" Many communities founded near mining areas became ghost towns when gold or silver deposits ran out, but some survived—Helena, Montana, began life as Last Chance Gulch—and the initial thrust into frontier areas by miners resulted in permanent occupation of new sections of the nation.

The last great strike in 1896 sent miners rushing to the Klondike in Alaska, a U.S. possession that had largely been ignored since being purchased from Russia in 1867 for a paltry $7.2 million. In fact when Secretary of State William H. Seward signed the treaty completing the sale on March 30,

1867, he was ridiculed for buying an area the *New York Tribune* described as consisting of mainly "impassable deserts of snow" and "inaccessible mountain ranges" and having no economic value except for "fishing and trading with the Indians." [106]

But "Seward's Folly" proved to be a bargain when gold was discovered there three decades later.

THE GREAT PLAINS

The search for gold and silver brought miners and settlers for the first time to the Great Plains, which had been neglected for decades because they were not believed to be fit for habitation by anyone except Native Americans. The Plains' inhospitable reputation came from early explorers like Zebulon Pike, who in 1806 first sighted and gave his name to Pikes Peak and nicknamed the Plains the "Great American Desert."

The Great Plains covered the present states of Oklahoma, Kansas, Nebraska, the Dakotas, most of Montana, and large parts of Wyoming and Colorado. The Plains' desert areas, dramatic buttes and stone formations, and rolling, grass-covered hills barren of trees seemed forbidding to Americans accustomed to forests, lush vegetation, and plentiful lakes and rivers. "The entire West," said historian Bernard De Voto, "was strange to the American eye. Nothing that the American people had known prepared them for it intellectually or emotionally." [107]

Public opinion mirrored comments like this one by Senator Daniel Webster, who in the 1830s said of the Great Plains and the Rocky Mountains:

> What do we want with the vast, worthless area, this region of savage and wild beasts, of deserts, of shifting sands, and whirlwinds of dust, of cactus and prairie dogs? To what use could we ever hope to put these great deserts or these endless mountain ranges, impenetrable and covered to their base with eternal snow? I will never vote one cent from the public treasury to place the Pacific coast one inch nearer to Boston than it now is. [108]

But when "Oregon fever," gold in California, and rich strikes elsewhere brought Americans into this region, they found it suitable for settlement. The growing numbers of newcomers, however, once again collided head-on with the land's original occupants.

INDIAN WARS

By 1847 Marcus and Narcissa Whitman had completed construction of their mission at Waiilatpu in present-day Oregon and were trying to Christianize the Cayuse tribe. That summer Narcissa wrote in her diary that Native Americans were bewildered by the growing flood of whites invading their land: "The poor Indians are amazed at the overwhelming numbers of Americans coming into the country. They seem not to know what to make of it." [109]

Indian tribes resented the white intruders, who not only took their land but

News Media and Westward Expansion

Newspapers and magazines played an important part in chronicling, promoting, and romanticizing the nation's Westward Expansion. In The Conquest of the West: A Sourcebook on the American West, *editor Carter Smith comments on the role the media played in this vital period in U.S. history.*

"The opening of the American West coincided with, and was in fact made possible by, a communication explosion in the United States. The number of newspapers published in the United States multiplied enormously in the opening years of the nineteenth century, providing a vast network carrying news from the frontier to the most civilized part of the East and back again. In the 1840s, illustrated magazines and weeklies became common, giving an added dimension to news reporting.

Another medium which came of age during this period, lithographing, also contributed to this explosion. This medium allowed the maps, political cartoons, portraits, and city views of the time to be produced far more quickly and cheaply than ever before. Lithography proved a versatile and valuable tool. Government expeditions surveying the West used it to reproduce for wide publication their detailed maps and drawings.

These images, becoming commonplace in American life, had a great impact on the way Easterners thought of the West, just as today, they help shape our historical perspective. While some were scientific and factual, others were clearly biased. The political cartoons were produced not by independent observers, but by artists for hire who were paid by or who sought favor with the political parties of the day. After the Civil War, the portrayal of the West became heavily romanticized in the illustrated reporting of such artists as Frederic Remington and others. It was in their drawings for magazines such as *Harper's Weekly* that the exploits of the cowboy, the gunslinger, and the U.S. Cavalry were first celebrated."

brought new diseases to which Native Americans had no immunity. Measles is a childhood disease that was a minor health problem for whites, who had built up an immunity to it through previous exposure. But in the summer and fall of 1847 an outbreak of measles killed hundreds of Indians in Oregon. When Cayuse Chief

Tilokaikt brought his three children to Whitman for medical attention and they died despite his care, the Cayuse attacked the mission on November 29, killed the Whitmans and seven others, and took fifty-one women and children into captivity.

The Whitman incident highlights one of the most devastating problems pioneers inflicted on Native Americans. Although it is estimated that only about 4,000 Indians and 7,000 whites were killed in direct warfare during a century of conflict that began in 1789, tens of thousands of Indians perished from measles, smallpox, cholera, and other diseases brought to their homelands. In 1820, for example, the Spanish province of California had about 130,000 Indians, but within a few decades disease reduced their numbers to only 30,000.

The Plains were now being crisscrossed by wagon trains and populated by settlers, who chased away or slaughtered buffalo and other prairie and mountain game that provided food for Native Americans. The result of the new mass migration in the 1850s was the most serious Indian conflict the country had experienced, three decades of raids and sporadic fighting up and down the western Plains.

The underlying cause was a total conflict in philosophy and lifestyles between the two sides, one that had existed since the first colonists came to America. Historian James West Davidson explains this cultural divide:

> What most separated white and Indian cultures were attitudes toward the land and all that was on it. Man, for the Indians, was not a transcendent being, but a single part of a complex web of animals, plants, and other natural elements—all with souls of their own. Where Europeans viewed nature as a resource to be exploited, the Indians saw it as sacred. [110]

Such reverence for the land gave Indians a religious loyalty to special places, and when whites trespassed on these sacred areas, incidents occurred that led to warfare. Also, as white settlers began pushing into marginal lands the federal government had set aside decades earlier for Indians, the government in 1851 introduced a policy of "concentration" in which it forced tribes to sign treaties that further limited the boundaries of their land. As with earlier treaties these agreements were supposed to be "forever," but they never were. When whites decided they needed more Indian land, the federal government simply forced tribes to accept new treaties that squeezed them into ever smaller and less desirable areas.

By 1862 the domain of the Santee Sioux along the Minnesota River had been whittled down to a strip 10 miles wide and 150 miles long. When the Minnesota frontier began to push into even this small area, the Sioux began raiding white settlements, killing more than six hundred people. When General John Pope was dispatched to subdue them, he told his officers, "They are to be treated as maniacs or wild beasts and by no means as people with whom treaties can be made." [111] Pope's forces defeated the warring Sioux and hanged thirty-eight warriors.

During a battle on the Rosebud River in Montana, Sioux warriors charge a detachment of soldiers.

There were massacres, however, on both sides. On June 4, 1864, when the bodies of a family of four that had been killed and mutilated by Indians were displayed in Denver, John M. Chivington, a minister, gathered a force of several hundred volunteers and set out to avenge them. On November 29 they came across an encampment of several hundred Cheyenne and a few Arapaho on Sand Creek in the southeastern part of the Colorado Territory. Without even knowing if the Indians were responsible for the deaths and without any warning, the vigilantes attacked, killing an estimated 300 Indians, including 225 women and children.

An interpreter with the volunteers who described the battle testified to the savagery of revengeful whites. "They were scalped, their brains knocked out; the men used their knives, ripped open women, clubbed little children, knocked them in the head with their guns, beat their brains out, mutilated their bodies in every sense of the word." [112]

The Sand Creek Massacre fueled the hatred and fighting spirit of Native Americans during this period of almost

A HISTORIC INDIAN GATHERING

In September 1851 the greatest gathering of Indian tribes in U.S. history occurred. Worried about attacks by hostile Indians as more and more settlers were passing through the Great Plains, the U.S. government had invited northern tribes to a meeting. The Sioux, Arikara, Shoshone, Cheyenne, Assinboine, Arapaho, and Gros Ventre were asked to allow pioneers to travel peacefully through their lands. The following account of this historic meeting is from The Mammoth Book of the West *by Jon E. Lewis:*

"Colonel Thomas Fitzpatrick addressed the tribesmen, telling them that the Great Father [the U.S. president] was 'aware that your buffalo and game are driven off, and your grass and timber consumed by the opening of roads and the passing of emigrants through your countries. For these losses he desires to compensate you.' The compensation offered the tribes was $50,000 a year, plus guns, if [they] would keep away from the trail and confine themselves to designated tracts of land. (Thus began the reservation system, though no one yet called it that.)

The Indians 'touched the pen,' and many went away in the belief that an age of harmony between the White and Red people was about to begin. Cut Nose of the Arapaho declared: 'I will go home satisfied. We have to live on these streams and in these hills, and I would be glad if the Whites would pick out a place for themselves and not come into our grounds.'"

Two years later a similar council was held with bands of the Comanche and Kiowa in Kansas. They agreed to refrain from molesting emigrants on the Santa Fe Trail in return for the annuity of eighteen thousand dollars in goods.

Lewis concluded by saying "the treaties were doomed to failure," not only because the chiefs did not have the power to speak for their entire tribes but also because of "the White men's failures," which included broken promises and new demands in the future for more Indian land.

constant warfare. But the campaign Pope started in Minnesota was the opening phase of a guerrilla war that would rage unabated until the final Plains tribes were conquered and the entire area controlled by whites.

COMMUNICATIONS AND TRANSPORTATION

The rapid growth of California and other far western areas led to two major problems—how the east could stay in communication with these new, distant Americans and how to transport people and material between the two coasts.

In 1848 it took thirty days to send mail via ship around Panama at the exorbitant cost of eighty cents an ounce. In 1856, seventy-five thousand Californians signed petitions to Congress demanding faster mail service, and two years later the federal government finally acted. On September 16, 1858, John Butterfield began fulfilling a government contract by carrying mail and passengers on the 2,795-mile trip between Tipton, Missouri, and San Francisco in the amazingly speedy time, for that era, of only twenty-five days.

When the first coach arrived in San Francisco a day ahead of schedule on Oc-

tober 10, the *San Francisco Bulletin* hailed Butterfield's "swift wagons" for a great achievement: "The importance of the enterprise cannot be too highly appreciated. California *is by it bound to the rest of the Union*." [113]

A quicker way to deliver mail appeared on April 3, 1860, with the start of the Pony Express. The daring riders who carried mail had answered the following ad: "WANTED: Young, skinny, wiry fellows not over 18. Must be expert riders willing to risk death daily. Orphans preferred." [114]

A string of pony riders could dash across the continent in ten days or less, changing horses at one of 190 way stations located at intervals of ten to fifteen miles. The express service was costly, up

In this painting by famed western artist Frederic Remington, a Pony Express rider dashes away after switching to a fresh horse.

to five dollars a half ounce, but speedy communication was vitally needed to keep both halves of the continent in touch.

The Pony Express lasted only until October 24, 1861, when the Pacific Telegraph Company and the Overland Telegraph Company put the brave, daring riders out of business by completing their transcontinental lines. Messages could now be sent in seconds instead of seven days and sixteen hours, the Express's record time to carry the text of Abraham Lincoln's inaugural address in March 1861. The first telegram from San Francisco to New York embodied the spirit of Manifest Destiny: "The Pacific to the Atlantic sends greetings; and may both oceans be dry before a foot of all that land that lies between them shall belong to any other than one united country." [115]

In 1855 the firm of Russell, Majors, and Waddell started a freight wagon service from St. Joseph, Missouri, to San Francisco. The company employed four thousand men and its thirty-five hundred wagons trundled vital supplies back and forth between east and west.

But the ultimate answer to transportation was an intercontinental railroad. When it was finally built after the Civil War, the railroad not only solved the problem of moving people and goods, it ignited the last great westward surge of people that would finally eliminate the American frontier.

6 Populating the Plains: Railroads, Cattle, and Farmers

When Abraham Lincoln was elected president in 1860, the same year Oregon was admitted to the Union as the thirty-third state, more than a third of America was still frontier. This huge, undeveloped area was divided into a half-dozen territories sandwiched between California and Oregon and the settled east, whose border ran in a straight line down America's midsection from Minnesota on the Canadian border all the way south to Louisiana on the Gulf of Mexico.

Lincoln was elected on a single issue—slavery—that divided the nation and led to civil war on April 12, 1861, when Confederate forces fired on Fort Sumter in South Carolina. The Republican president would lead the North to victory over the South to free African Americans, but a program he signed into law in May 1862 would have an almost equally dramatic impact on the nation's future.

On February 1, 1861, two months before the start of the nation's most tragic war, Lincoln backed the Homestead Act, which offered people 160 acres of western land free just for living on it for five years. Lincoln stated "I am in favor of settling the wild lands into small parcels so that every poor man may have a home."[116] The

simplicity of eligibility to receive free land was the act's strong point: "Any person who is the head of a family, or who has arrived at the age of twenty-one years, and is a citizen of the United States, or who

President Abraham Lincoln helped make it easier for settlers to own their own land.

shall have filed his declaration of intention to become such."[117]

The lure of free land was so strong that even during the perilous period of the Civil War, three hundred thousand people moved west, and by 1864 the generous new law had put some 1.26 million acres into the hands of settlers. Three new states had also been admitted to the Union—Kansas (1861), West Virginia (1863), and Nevada (1864).

In an 1864 *New York Tribune* editorial, Horace Greeley offered the nation a bit of advice that would sum up the dramatic Westward Expansion of the next three decades: "Go West, young man, and grow up with the country."[118] The famous phrase was originally penned in 1851 by L. B. Soule, a Terre Haute, Indiana, newspaper editor, but Greeley has always been linked with it because millions of people read it first in his publication.

Americans, especially poor immigrants who poured into the country following the war, took the advice to heart, flowing west to tame more new land in the final years of the nineteenth century than had been settled in all of America's past. Surging into Kansas and Nebraska, North and South Dakota, Montana, Wyoming, and other parts of the wild, unknown Great Plains, these hardy pioneers by 1890 would eliminate the American frontier.

RAILROADS

One of the main forces powering this final westward migration was construction of the first intercontinental railroad, which not only linked both sides of the vast continent but helped populate the huge frontier nestled between the two settled coasts. Historian Frederick Jackson Turner wrote at the end of the nineteenth century that the railroad was the final key transportation development in Westward Expansion: "The buffalo trail became the Indian trail, and this became the 'trader's trace'; the trails widened into roads and the roads into turnpikes and these in turn were transformed into railroads."[119]

America had only thirty-five thousand miles of railroad lines when the Civil War ended in 1865. By 1900 that figure had multiplied five times, and the nation had more miles of track than all of Europe. In 1862 Congress chose the Central Pacific to build the transcontinental line eastward from San Francisco and the Union Pacific to lay track west from Omaha, Nebraska.

As it had been for many Americans who moved west, the incentive for railroad officials to tackle the immense, extremely difficult project was greed: for every mile of track they laid, the two companies received at least twenty sections of land along the route, and forty sections in areas where construction was most difficult, such as through mountain passes. One section equaled ten square miles, and the two railroads combined received 45 million acres of prime land, which they sold at huge profits. Twenty years later, rail magnates like William H. Vanderbilt arrogantly boasted of their profits: "The railroads are not run for the benefit of the public. That cry is all nonsense. They are built for men who invested their money and expected to get a fair percentage on the same."[120]

Construction of the cross-country rail line was one of the nation's greatest post–Civil War accomplishments. It began on July 10, 1865, when workers hammered the first rail into place at Omaha, Nebraska. Ten thousand Chinese immigrants hired by the Central Pacific and thousands of Irish taken on by the Union Pacific labored with thousands of other workers from many other countries to lay track across the plains, over mountains, and through arid desert. Swinging heavy sledgehammers an estimated 21 million times to pound in the spikes needed to secure the rails the trains would ride upon—there were ten spikes per rail and four hundred rails for every mile of track—these workers forged an iron path across eighteen hundred miles of wilderness.

The two railroads pushed their crews unmercifully as both fought to lay more track so they could claim more free land, but Congress and President Ulysses S. Grant finally ended the race for riches by deciding the two lines should connect at Promontory, Utah. On May 10, 1869, when railroad officials hammered in ceremonial gold and silver spikes to secure the final rail, a telegrapher sent out a one-word message that brought joy to millions of Americans: "Done."[121]

By 1883 three more rail lines connected East and West. One, the Southern Pacific from New Orleans to Los Angeles, traveled over land acquired in the Gadsden Purchase—on December 30, 1853, the United States paid Mexico $10 million for twenty-nine thousand square miles of land that today makes up the southern parts of Arizona and New Mexico. The deal that completed the borders of what are now the forty-eight contiguous states was made partly because the land was considered a good route for a future transcontinental railroad.

In addition to carrying people, mail, and products more quickly, cheaply, and efficiently than any other means of transportation, railroads, nicknamed "the modern ship of the Plains," made it easier for people to settle frontier areas. Towns grew up quickly around train stations dotting the rail lines, and these communities provided settlers with vital supplies, entertainment, churches, schools, and law enforcement to help make their lives better.

THE CATTLE KINGDOM

For many people, the cowboy is the most enduring symbol of the American West. Who, after all, has not heard a western singer croon "Home on the Range," the song whose lyrics helped define the romance of the cowboy. But the cowboy and the cattle industry that employed him had a fairly brief heyday, one that was linked to the coming of the railroad to the Great Plains.

In the 1830s when Americans began populating the Mexican province of Texas, it was already home to thousands of cattle, courtesy of Spanish conquerors who brought them along for food. By 1865 some 5 million cattle roamed the plains, many of them free for the taking for anyone brave enough to tangle with the longhorned beasts.

DRIVING THE GOLDEN SPIKE

This account by Alexander Toponce, who witnessed the historic completion of the transcontinental railroad, is found in Gary Noy's Distant Horizon: Documents from the Nineteenth-Century American West.

"I saw the golden spike driven. On the last day only about 100 feet [of rails] were laid, and everyone tried to have a hand in the work. I took a shovel from an Irishman, and threw a shovel full of dirt on the ties just to tell about it afterward. When they came to drive the last spike, Governor [Leland] Stanford [of California], president of the Central Pacific, took the sledge, and the first time he struck he missed the spike and hit the rail. What a howl went up! Irish, Chinese, Mexicans, and everybody yelled with delight, 'He missed it. Yee.' Then Stanford tried it again and tapped the spike and the telegraph operators had fixed their instruments so that the tap was reported in all the offices east and west, and set bells to tapping in hundreds of towns and cities. Then vice president T. C. Durant of the Union Pacific took up the sledge and he missed the spike the first time. Then everybody slapped everybody else again and yelled, 'He missed it too, Yow!'"

On May 10, 1869, railroad workers and officials, dignitaries, and others gather at Promontory, Utah, to celebrate completion of the first transcontinental railroad.

After the Civil War, when growing populations in northern cities needed more beef, Texas ranchers began to collect huge herds and drive them hundreds of miles to railheads like Abilene, Texas, and Dodge City, Kansas, where the animals were sold and shipped east. Ranchers herded cattle to market along the Chisholm, Pecos, Goodnight, and Bozeman Trails, fighting bad weather, a lack of water, rustlers, and Indians who tried to steal their stock. By 1871 some 1.5 million cattle a year were pouring into Abilene, and profits were so big that within a decade the cattle industry had spread northward over the Great Plains all the way to Montana.

In *The Shaping of the American Past*, Robert Kelley explains why the cattle industry grew so quickly: "A veritable 'gold rush' set in for western ranch land. The road to wealth seemed ridiculously easy. A man had only to buy some animals, wait a few years while they multiplied on free government grazing land, and he was rich." [122]

The formula worked for a while, but by the mid 1880s the Great Plains began to be overpopulated with cattle and grass began to be scarce. A severe winter in 1885 killed hundreds of thousands of animals, bankrupting many ranchers. The open range phase of the cattle industry soon ended, and from 1886 to 1895 the

Workers force cattle up a chute and into a railroad boxcar. Stockyard scenes like this in Abilene, Kansas, were common during the 1870s.

number of cattle declined from 9 million to 3 million.

In addition to bad weather and increased competition, the cattle business was also curbed by the arrival of thousands of farmers who came to make their homes on the Plains.

THE FARM INVASION

In the last four decades of the nineteenth century, three times as much land was turned to farming as in the previous two centuries. Historian James West Davidson describes this farm explosion:

> In the 1860s they had come in the trickles; in the 1870s they became a torrent. They were farmers from the East and Midwest, black freedmen from the South, and immigrants from Europe. What bound them together was a hunger for land based on their rural and peasant backgrounds. The number of farms in the United States increased from around two million on the eve of the Civil War to almost six million in 1890. [123]

Farmers angered ranchers by living on government-owned land where the ranchers had previously grazed their cattle and erecting barbed wire fences to keep the animals from the prairie grass they had once fed upon for free. Ranchers derogatorily referred to farmers as "nesters" and "sodbusters," the latter nickname coming from the thick sod that covered the prairies and was difficult to till. Farmers were not able to make their homes on the plains until steel-bladed plows that could slice through the tough prairie turf became available. The railroad lines also made it more economically feasible to settle new areas by providing farmers a way to ship their products to various markets.

These hardy newcomers figured out a practical use for the sod that gave them so much trouble—they cut it into huge chunks to build homes in areas that had little timber, which was normally used in housing construction. Historian James West Davidson describes this style of prairie accommodations:

> For poor families, life on the Plains meant a sod house or a dugout carved out of the hillside for protection from the wind. Tough, root-bound sod was cut into bricks about a foot wide and three feet long and laid edgewise to create walls three feet thick; sod bricks were laid over rafters for a roof. The average house was seldom more than 18 by 24 feet and in severe weather it had to accommodate animals as well as people. A sod house had the advantage of being cheap, too heavy to blow away in the wind, and too wet to catch fire. The thick walls kept the house warm in winter and cool in summer. In the spring wildflowers and grass turned the roof into a small garden. [124]

However, heavy rain could collapse the roof or allow mud and water to seep into the living area, wooden floors were an uncommon luxury, and sod house dwellers

THE COWBOY MYTH

The myth of the cowboy is one of the clearest, strongest, and most romantic to emerge from the varied history of America's Westward Expansion. The cowboy's wide-brimmed ten-gallon hat, leather boots with spurs that jingle-jangled musically as he walked, and ornamental belt buckle are all worn today by people throughout the world who have never seen a real beef steer much less thought of roping one; they are simply in love with the image.

In Visions of the American West, *Gerald F. Kreyche writes of this stereotype:*

"Without question, the archetypal image of the cowboy is the most romantic and longest lasting mythic image to come out of America. The myth, although grounded in reality, probably began with the pulp magazines popular in the 1870s. There, the cowboy image was bigger than life and typified virility, action, excitement, freedom, loyalty, egalitarianism, independence, quiet determination, and competence."

However, the image of the cowboy most people have today, based as it is mostly on the exploits of movie stars ranging from John Wayne to Clint Eastwood, is more myth than fact. Most movies fail to show that many of the first cowboys were Mexican, that many African Americans drove cattle, and that women also rode the cattle trails. Westward Expansion: An Eyewitness History, *includes this account by Amanda Banks, who drove cattle to market from Texas in the 1870s:*

"We had no unpleasant experiences with the Indians, although they came to camp and tried to trade with the men. We narrowly escaped having trouble with a couple of what we supposed to be rustlers. While alone in camp one afternoon, two men came up and were throwing rocks in among the grazing cattle. I called to them to stop and said, 'Don't you know you'll stampede those cattle,' and they answered, 'That's what we're trying to do.' Just then some of the men rode up and the rustlers left hurriedly."

had to battle flies, gnats, mosquitoes, and a lack of light. Even so, for many pioneers the "soddie" provided adequate, if primitive, shelter and allowed them to survive their first few difficult years on the frontier.

INDIANS AND SETTLERS CLASH

At the end of the Civil War about 225,000 Native Americans inhabited the Rocky Mountains and Great Plains west of Kansas and Nebraska. The railroad lines

U.S. troops overwhelm a group of Cheyenne Indians during a battle near Fort Robinson, Nebraska.

that began to snake across their ancestral land became a dark omen of the final, tragic chapter in their battle with whites for control of the continent.

The iron rails unleashed a large-scale invasion by ranchers, farmers, and other settlers into the vast area that treaties had set aside for Native Americans. When settlers started moving onto these lands, they found that the Sioux, Apache, Arapaho, Cheyenne, Comanche, Kiowa, Nez Percé, and other Plains tribes were fierce fighters. Unlike their eastern counterparts, Plains Indians rode horses—descendants of animals the Spanish brought to the New World in the seventeenth century. Historian Alan Axelrod claims the introduction of horses dramatically transformed the lifestyles of many tribes by making them better hunters and fighters:

The horse revolutionized Plains life, making the buffalo hunt and warfare more efficient and more demanding of skill and daring. The gain in efficiency allowed the hunter-warrior more leisure time, and by the end of the eighteenth century, when horse culture was at its early height, Plains tribes developed elaborate war games and religious rites; the horses had, in effect, liberated Plains culture. [125]

Clashes with Native Americans intensified during the Civil War, and when the conflict was over, the U.S. Army decided to subdue them once and for all. General of the Army William T. Sherman—whose middle name, ironically, was Tecumseh, after the famed Shawnee Indian chief—put General Philip H. Sheridan in charge of defending the West.

For the next decade these two famous generals directed a force of more than twenty-three thousand soldiers in the fight to eliminate Native American opposition. About 20 percent of the soldiers were African Americans, nicknamed "buffalo soldiers" by Native Americans who thought the soldiers' hair resembled the coarse hide of the buffalo.

The mindset that guided Sherman can be seen in his instructions to Sheridan in 1868 after bands of warriors attacked settlements and stagecoach stations: "The more we can kill this year the less will have to be killed in the next war, for the more I see of these Indians the more convinced I am that they all have to be killed or be maintained as a species of paupers." Acting partly out of concern to protect the vital new intercontinental railroad inching its way across the Plains, Sherman the next day told Union Pacific officials, "I hope not an Indian will be left in that belt of country through which the two railroads pass." [126]

Sherman could not have found a more eager subordinate than Sheridan, who once uttered the famous but disturbing phrase: "The only good Indian is a dead

When a thundering herd of buffalo halts this railroad train, workers and passengers shoot the great shaggy beasts.

Indian."[127] And Sheridan knew that one way to kill Indians was to deny them food.

PLIGHT OF THE INDIANS

The millions of buffalo that once roamed the Great Plains were the main source of food for many Indians, who also used buffalo hides to build teepees. But to railroad executives, cattle ranchers, and farmers, the huge, woolly animals were simply a nuisance, and when their hides became popular in leather making, hunters began slaughtering them by the millions.

From 1872 to 1874 some 9 million were killed, and by 1883 the bison, still an enduring symbol today of America's frontier past, was nearly extinct. Little Robe, a Cheyenne chief, voiced the concerns of all the Plains tribes when he complained: "Your people make big talk, and sometimes make war, if an Indian kills a white man's ox to keep his wife and children from starving; what do you think my people ought to say when they see their [buffalo] killed by your race when you are not hungry?"[128]

Native Americans were appalled and angry that hide hunters shot hundreds of buffalo in a few days and left the meat to rot while Indian families went hungry. But Sheridan encouraged the slaughter, and when Texas considered legislation to protect the state's remaining buffalo, he went to Austin to protest:

The buffalo hunters have done more in two years to settle the vexed Indian question than the entire U.S. army has done in ten years. They are destroying the Indian commissary. Send them powder and lead if you will, but for the sake of helping [white] people, let them kill, skin and sell until the buffalo are exterminated.[129]

In addition to being denied game they needed to live, Native Americans were being forced to live in smaller and smaller areas. Even federal officials sent to help them betrayed them. In 1864 the Indian agent for the Osage tribe in Kansas declared, "The Indian lands are the best in the state and justice would demand, as will every consideration of policy and humanity, that these fertile lands be thrown open to settlement [by] civilized and industrious [white] men." [130]

That attitude allowed white settlers to trespass continually on lands previously declared off-limits to any but Native Americans. By 1871 the Shoshone and Bannock of Idaho had been pushed off land promised them in treaties, and by 1873 the Crow and Ute in Colorado had lost most of their territory, with the Ute surrendering four million acres.

But Great Plains tribes like the Sioux, Cheyenne, and Arapaho kept fighting, and in 1876 Native Americans scored their most famous victory over white soldiers.

CUSTER'S LAST STAND

In 1874 Lieutenant Colonel George Armstrong Custer, a Civil War hero nicknamed the "Glory Hunter" by one of his

SITTING BULL

Sitting Bull (Tatanka Yotanka), chief of the Hunkpapa band of Sioux, is one of the best-known Native Americans, both because of his participation in "Custer's Last Stand" and the fame he gained as a member of Buffalo Bill Cody's traveling Wild West Show. His life was also a microcosm of the injustices done to Native Americans in the cause of Westward Expansion.

In *The Westerners*, historian Dee Brown explains that Sitting Bull understood what was happening even as he vainly tried to fight the white onslaught that would reduce his people to the status of beggars on the land they once proudly roamed. "Let us alone. Let us alone. We want only to be left alone," he said when miners and white settlers began invading the Black Hills, which were sacred to the Sioux.

Sitting Bull did not want to fight whites, but he found confinement to a reservation intolerable. When U.S. troops searched out his band after they fled the reservation, Sitting Bull had no choice but to fight. After the victory Sitting Bull and his band of Sioux escaped to Canada in the spring of 1877, but within four years they were forced to return to the great Sioux Reservation in South Dakota because they had no money or food. "I wish it to be remembered," Sitting Bull said, "that I was the last man of my tribe to surrender my rifle."

Sitting Bull was imprisoned until 1883 and then sent to the Standing Rock Reservation and taught to farm, something he hated. "It is your own doing that we are here," he complained to reservation officials, who often shortchanged the Sioux on promised food and supplies. "You sent us here and asked us to live as you do, and it is not right for us to live in poverty."

In 1885 he joined Cody's Wild West Show, becoming world famous as he toured eastern cities and the major capitals of Europe, but within a few years he returned to the reservation, living in a log cabin because there were no buffalo hides to make traditional teepees. In the summer of 1889 when government agencies bullied individual Sioux to sign treaties giving away more of their land, Sitting Bull refused.

Reservation officials placed him in jail because they feared he would cause trouble, but later released him. At daybreak on December 15, 1890, forty-five Sioux dressed in agency police uniforms came to arrest him. Sitting Bull submitted quietly, but when he stepped out of his cabin they opened fire, killing him.

biographers, led an expedition into the Black Hills of South Dakota, the *Paha Sapa* territory that was sacred to the Sioux. The trip was a violation of an 1868 treaty that promised whites would keep off the land, but when Custer returned and reported the area had gold deposits "from the grass roots down,"[131] no treaty could hold back whites crazed by the lust for gold.

When prospectors and others began to invade Sioux territory illegally, even a *Chicago Tribune* journalist named John Finerty, who referred to Native Americans in his stories as "savages," was troubled by the nation's failure to keep its promises:

> The white man's government might make what treaties it pleases with the Indians, but it was quite a different matter to get the white man himself to respect the official parchment. Three-fourths of the Black Hills region, and all of the Big Horn, were barred by the Great Father [the U.S. president] and Sitting Bull against the daring and acquisitive Caucasian race. [But when Custer] confirmed reports of gold finds, thereafter, a wall of fire, not to mention a wall of Indians, could not stop the encroachments of that terrible white race. [132]

When the Sioux and Cheyenne began to fight back against invading whites, the Department of the Interior decided to renege on its treaties and ordered all northern Plains tribes to report to Indian agencies by January 31, 1876. When not all the tribes obeyed, President Grant ordered the military to take action against Native Americans still in the disputed

Lieutenant Colonel George Armstrong Custer (top) and his men are surrounded by Sioux and Cheyenne warriors in the battle known as "Custer's Last Stand."

area, a territory that had been promised to them forever.

In June, Custer was leading one of two columns of soldiers under the command of General Alfred Terry. Custer and his Seventh Cavalry arrived at the Little Bighorn River on June 24, and the next day he decided to attack a huge Indian encampment that was close by, even though his Indian scouts advised against it.

Knowing how many enemy warriors faced them, the Indian scouts began singing their death songs. But Custer, hungry for glory, merely said, "The largest Indian camp on the North American continent is ahead and I'm going to attack it." [133]

Facing more than two thousand Cheyenne and Sioux led by famous chiefs such as Crazy Horse and Sitting Bull, Custer made a foolish tactical decision. In an attempt to encircle the Indian encampment, Custer split his force into three parts. Left with only two to three hundred men, Custer's force was nearly helpless when an overwhelming number of Indians attacked, wiping out his troops in a battle that lasted about an hour. The only survivor was Comanche, a cavalry horse who for many years afterward appeared in parades, saddled but riderless.

The battle—remembered as "Custer's Last Stand" by whites and "The Battle of the Greasy Grass" by the Sioux—was the most famous Native American victory in their long wars with whites. Following is an account by Two Moon, a Cheyenne chief who fought at the Little Big Horn:

> Then the Sioux rode up the ridge on all sides, riding very fast. The Cheyennes went up the left way. Then the shooting was quick, quick. Pop-pop-pop—very fast. Some of the soldiers were down on their knees, some standing, officers all in front. The smoke was like a great cloud, and everywhere the Sioux went the dust rose like smoke, we circled all around them—swirling like water around a stone. We shoot, we ride fast, we shoot again. Soldiers drop, and horses fall on them. Soldiers in line drop, but one man rides up and down the line—all the time shooting. He rode a sorrel horse, with white legs and white forelegs. I don't know who he was. He was a brave man. [134]

Joy over the victory was short-lived. Outraged and humiliated by this defeat on the eve of the nation's Centennial celebration, the U.S. Army poured troops into the area and by late summer had split the Sioux and Cheyenne into small, harmless bands. In September Crazy Horse was arrested and taken to Fort Cloud, where he was bayoneted to death while allegedly trying to escape. The defiant tribes were all forced to surrender and return to Indian land set aside for them, but they were barred from their beloved *Paha Sapa.*

Chief Sitting Bull escaped to Canada briefly with a small group of Sioux, but in 1877 they were forced to return to the

The somber face of Sioux chief Sitting Bull conveys the sadness of all Native Americans who lost their homes and freedom.

Guthrie, Oklahoma: Built in One Day

An old saying claims "Rome was built in a day." It wasn't, but Guthrie, Oklahoma, was.

On April 22, 1889, when Indian Territory was opened for settlement, tens of thousands of people took trains to areas that had already been mapped out as new towns. In Eyewitness to the American West: From the Aztec Empire to the Digital Frontier in the Words of Those Who Saw It Happen, *editor David Colbert includes this account by* Harper's Weekly *writer William Howard of how Guthrie was created in a single day.*

"Unlike Rome the city of Guthrie was built in a day. To be strictly accurate in the matter, it might be said that it was built in an afternoon. At twelve o'clock on Monday, April 22, the resident population of Guthrie was nothing; before sundown it was at least ten thousand. In that time streets had been laid out, town lots staked off, and steps taken toward the formation of a municipal government. At twilight the campfires for ten thousand people gleamed on the grassy slopes of the Cimarron Valley, where, the night before, the coyote, the gray wolf, and the deer had roamed undisturbed.

Never before in the history of the West has so large a number of people been concentrated in one place in so short a time. To the conservative Eastern man, who is wont to see cities grow by decades, the settlement of Guthrie was magical beyond belief, to the quick-acting resident of the West, it was merely a particularly lively townsite speculation.

It is estimated that between six and seven thousand persons reached Guthrie by train from the north the first afternoon, and that fully three thousand came in by wagon from the north and east, and by train from the South, thus making a total population for the first day of about ten thousand."

Sioux reservation. It was also in 1877 that Nez Percé Chief Joseph—his Indian name was Inmuttooyahlatlat—staged a remarkable rebellion against the federal government. When his band of eight hundred was ordered to leave its home in Oregon and move to a small reservation, like Sitting Bull he decided to take his tribe to Canada, where he thought they could live in freedom.

For four months Chief Joseph led U.S. soldiers on a wild two thousand-mile chase across Oregon, Washington, Idaho, and Montana, outmaneuvering pursuing troops that outnumbered his warriors by at least ten times and defeating them several times in battle. But Chief Joseph finally had to surrender on October 5 when troops led by General Nelson A. Miles surrounded the Nez Percé near the Bear Paw Mountains of Montana, just forty miles shy of the Canadian border.

His words that day are among the most tragic ever spoken by an Indian leader: "Hear me, my chiefs, I am tired; my heart is sick and sad. From where the sun now stands, I will fight no more forever."[135] Although he had been promised he could return home, Chief Joseph and his band were sent to a barren reservation in Indian Territory (later Oklahoma) where many became ill and died.

The last Indian wars centered around the Apache. The surrender of Geronimo in 1886 after he had waged a long guerrilla war against U.S. soldiers ended attempts by Native Americans to fight back. "Once I moved about like the wind. Now I surrender to you and that is all,"[136] the sixty-year-old Apache leader told General George Crook.

THE OKLAHOMA LAND RUSH

The final land grab by white settlers came in 1889. President Benjamin Harrison, who had been inaugurated less than two months earlier as the nation's twenty-third president, opened up to white settlement a large portion of Indian Territory in what would become the state of Oklahoma in 1907. This land had been set aside for the Five Civilized Tribes six decades earlier and in the years since had become a dumping ground for other tribes pushed off their lands.

On April 22, 1889, some one hundred thousand people in wagons, carriages, and buckboards, on horses and mules, and even on foot, raced across a starting line to claim portions of 2 million acres of Indian land. The following account of the mad dash was written by William W. Howard for *Harper's Weekly* magazine:

> As the expectant home-seekers waited with restless patience, the clear, sweet notes of a cavalry bugle rose and hung a moment upon the startled air. It was noon. The last barrier of savagery in the United States was broken down. Moved by the same impulse, each driver lashed his horses furiously; each rider dug his spurs into his willing steed, and each man on foot caught his breath hard and darted forward. A cloud of dust rose where the home-seekers had stood in line, and when it had drifted away before the gentle breeze, the horses and wagons and men were tearing across the open country like fiends.[137]

America's final frontier had been breached. Manifest Destiny was reality.

The Legacy of the American Frontier

The tidal wave of Manifest Destiny did not stop at the Pacific Ocean. In 1893 it took one more final, giant leap of twenty-four hundred miles across the Pacific to the Hawaiian Islands after U.S. diplomat John L. Stevens sent this message to Washington from Honolulu: "The Hawaiian pear is now fully ripe and this is the golden hour for the United States to pluck it."[138]

America had coveted Hawaii since the end of the eighteenth century, when U.S. whaling and trading ships began stopping there for supplies; in the nineteenth century it had also become an important port for Far East trade and a source of sugar, a rich crop U.S. firms controlled. By 1893 American businessmen had taken control of Hawaii, wielding most of their power through an elected Assembly.

In 1891, Queen Liliuokalani had succeeded her brother, King Kalakaua, and begun moving to give Hawaiians more rights and win back control of their own land. By this time disease brought by whites had reduced the native Hawaiian population from about 250,000 at the start of the century to only 60,000, a health disaster similar to that which devastated Native Americans on the U.S. mainland.

Afraid that Liliuokalani would succeed, a self-constituted Committee of Safety headed by Sanford B. Dole and others involved in the sugar trade engineered the queen's overthrow with help from U.S. officials. On January 17, 1893, Stevens

Hawaiian Queen Liliuokalani, who in 1893 was overthrown in a takeover led by American businessmen.

ordered 150 marines from the cruiser *Boston* to protect American lives because of the threat of riots by Hawaiians, a threat that was nonexistent.

The Committee declared a provisional government headed by Dole and imprisoned Liliuokalani in the Iolani Palace. To avoid having her followers killed in a battle she knew they could not win, the queen surrendered:

> I do, under protest and impelled by [armed soldiers], yield my authority until such time as the government of the United States shall, upon the facts being presented to it, undo the action and reinstate me in the authority which I claim as the constitutional sovereign of the Hawaiian islands. [139]

President Grover Cleveland knew Hawaii had been illegally seized and refused to grant the provisional government's request for annexation. But in 1898, when Hawaii proved its value as a military port during the Spanish American War, Congress did annex it as a territory. On August 21, 1959, Hawaii became the fiftieth state.

THE FRONTIER SHAPES AMERICA

The Westward Expansion Thomas Jefferson envisioned taking place over a thousand years lasted less than a century, but the effects of this epic mass migration still linger today.

In 1893 University of Wisconsin Professor Frederick Jackson Turner presented a paper to the American Historical Society

Historian Frederick Jackson Turner, whose theory on how the frontier shaped America's development influenced the study of U.S. history for many decades.

in Chicago, Illinois, that revolutionized the study of U.S. history. He theorized that the character of Americans and their institutions, such as public schools which offered everyone a free education, were shaped by the nation's frontier experience, chiefly its nearly unlimited freedom and economic opportunities. Turner wrote that the U.S. Census for 1890 included this significant statement: "Up to and including 1880 the country had a frontier of settlement, but at present the unsettled area has been so broken into by isolated bodies of settlement that there can hardly be said to be a frontier line."[140]

The term "frontier" was defined in this era as any area with fewer than two residents per square mile. Turner theorized that life on the frontier, which he characterized as "the meeting point between savagery and civilization," changed not only the people who lived there, but the entire nation:

> Up to our own day America has been in a large degree the history of the colonization of the Great West. American social development has been continually beginning over again on the frontier. This perennial rebirth, this fluidity of American life, this expansion westward with new opportunities, furnish the forces dominating American character. The true point of view in the history of this nation is not the Atlantic Coast, it is the Great West. Even the slavery struggle occupies its important place in American history because of its relation to westward expansion. [141]

The frontier experience, Turner claimed, imbued America with characteristics that helped make it great: individuality, ingenuity, self-reliance, tolerance, openness to new ideas, energy to accomplish any task, the will to work for good instead of evil. He maintained that "these traits, while softening down, still persist" [142] in the nation's spirit.

One example of the positive effect of the frontier experience was the increased freedom women won, including the right to vote. In 1869 the Wyoming Territory became the first governmental body to allow women to vote, something the federal government denied women until 1920. In *The Westerners*, Dee Brown writes that frontier women improved their status by showing they could be as capable as men:

> In the quarter century after 1850, Western women burst loose from centuries of restrictive laws and customs, flaunting their new-found freedoms and accelerating a movement which is still spreading around the world. They invaded domains long held sacred by males—politics, the professions, even outlawry—and did it with such gentle deftness that the kingpins who held these bastions were barely aware of what was happening. [143]

THE DARK SIDE OF MANIFEST DESTINY

But Westward Expansion had its dark side. Historian James West Davidson notes that racism was one of the major assumptions underlying Manifest Destiny:

> The same belief in racial superiority that was used to justify Indian removal under [President Andrew] Jackson, to uphold slavery in the south, and to excuse segregation in the north also proved handy to defend expansion westward. The United States had a duty to regenerate the backward peoples of America, declared politicians and propagandists. [144]

This racism was revealed in the contempt many Americans felt for Mexicans, full-scale warfare directed against Native Americans, and the brutal reception given to Chinese immigrants who began coming to America in the second half of the nineteenth century. In *The American West: The Pictorial Epic of A Continent*, Lucius Beebe and Charles Clegg write:

> From the very beginning the Chinese brought trouble with them. The race prejudice of whites in California which had hitherto been directed against Mexicans and Indians, was extended to include the yellow race. Their manners, habits, language, religion and personalities incited prejudice, but their greatest crime was economic: they would work harder for longer hours and less wages than any white man and for this their lives were made miserable for decades.[145]

African Americans, however, were often accepted in the West. They played a large role in Westward Expansion, from mountain man James Beckwourth down to settlers who answered the call of the *Colored Citizen*, an African American paper that in March 29, 1879, urged freed slaves to move to Kansas: "If they come here and starve, all well and good. It is better to starve to death in Kansas then be shot and killed in the south."[146]

It should also be remembered that greed was one of the most compelling forces that sent Americans hurtling westward. In *Letters on America* in the 1830s, Michael Chevalier said of settlers in the Old Northwest Territory: "The motto of a western man is 'to conquer or die,' but

This illustration symbolizes the relentless Westward Expansion that created a nation from "sea to shining sea."

conquering with him means to make money; to build up a fortune from nothing, to buy lots at Chicago, Cleveland, or at St. Louis, and to sell them the next year at the rate of a thousand *per cent*. [147]

Westward Expansion involved a feverish rush to accumulate wealth, from prospectors seeking gold to railroad executives given millions of acres of land to connect the continent. The frontier they encountered was so vast and rich in natural resources that they believed it could never be exhausted. Historian Dee Brown claims this led to a wasteful attitude that harmed the environment:

> The west was there to be exploited and in the accomplishment of this, in their march to the Western Sea, they [mountain men] and many of the thousands who followed them destroyed a native civilization and obliterated innumerable species of animals and birds. They ripped apart the delicate balance of Plains grassland, they gutted mountains for metals, they leveled forests and created wastelands. They raped, stripped, and plundered land [once held sacred and revered by Native Americans]. [148]

A GREAT ACCOMPLISHMENT

But even though Westward Expansion led to problems Americans are still dealing with today, from the destruction of Native American culture to environmental concerns, the creation of a nation was a magnificent accomplishment. In 1844 an American politician infected with the vision of Manifest Destiny had bellowed: "Make way for the young American Buffalo—he has not yet got land enough. We will give him Oregon for his 'summer shade,' Texas 'as his winter pasture,' and 'the use of two oceans—the mighty Pacific and the turbulent Atlantic' to quench his thirst." [149]

It was an arrogant, selfish boast. But it was one that millions of men and women suffered, sweated, sacrificed, and even died to fulfill, and it stands as one of the greatest collective accomplishments Americans have ever shared.

Notes

Introduction: History's "Greatest Migration"

1. Quoted in Leonard Wibberley, *Young Man from the Piedmont: The Youth of Thomas Jefferson*. New York: Ariel Books, 1963, p.13.

2. Quoted in Frederick Merk, *History of the Westward Movement*. New York: Alfred A. Knopf, 1978, p. 616.

3. Quoted in Merk, *History of the Westward Movement*, p. 616.

4. Quoted in Carroll C. Calkins, ed., *The Story of America*. Pleasantville, NY: Readers Digest, 1975, p. 82.

5. Quoted in Marshall B. Davidson, *Life in America*, vol. 1. Boston: Hougton Mifflin, 1951, p. 157.

6. Quoted in Richard D. Heffner, *A Documentary History of the United States*. Bloomington: Indiana University Press, 1952, p. 170.

7. Quoted in Sanford Wexler, *Westward Expansion: An Eyewitness History*. New York: Facts On File, 1991, p. 158.

8. Quoted in Heffner, *A Documentary History of the United States*, p. 166.

Chapter 1: Adventurous Colonists Brave the Wilderness

9. Quoted in Davidson, *Life in America*, p. 164.

10. Quoted in David Colbert, ed., *Eyewitness to the American West: From the Aztec Empire to the Digital Frontier in the Words of Those Who Saw It Happen*. New York: Viking, 1998, p. 55.

11. Quoted in Allan Nevins, Henry Steele Commager, with Jeffrey Morris, *A Pocket History of the United States*, 9th ed. New York: Pocket Books, 1992, p. 28.

12. Quoted in Davidson, *Life in America*, p. 161.

13. Quoted in Robert Kelley, *The Shaping of the American Past: To 1877*, 5th ed. Englewood Cliffs, NJ: Prentice Hall, 1990, p. 90.

14. Quoted in Thomas Fleming, *Liberty! The American Revolution*. New York: Penguin, 1998, p. 355.

15. Quoted in Calkins, *The Story of America*, p. 69.

16. Quoted in Davidson, *Life in America*, p. 179.

17. Quoted in Wexler, *Westward Expansion*, p. 29.

18. Quoted in Michael Kraus, *The United States to 1865*. Ann Arbor: University of Michigan Press, 1969, p. 301.

19. Samuel Eliot Morison, *The Oxford History of the American People*. New York: Oxford University Press, 1965, p. 346.

20. Quoted in Wexler, *Westward Expansion*, p. 52.

21. Quoted in James West Davidson et al., *Nation of Nations: A Narrative History of the American Republic*, 2d ed. New York: McGraw-Hill, 1994, p. 46.

22. Winthrop D. Jordan, Miriam Greenblatt, and John S. Bowes, *The Americans: The History of a People and a Nation*. Evanston, IL: McDouglas, Little, 1985, p. 76.

23. Bernard De Voto, *Across the Wide Missouri*. Boston: Houghton Mifflin, 1947, p. 12

24. Quoted in Davidson et al., *Nation of Nations*, p. 317

25. Quoted in Wexler, *Westward Expansion*, p. 22.

26. Quoted in Wexler, *Westward Expansion*, p. 59.

27. Quoted in Davidson et al., *Nation of Nations*, p. 317.

28. Quoted in Alvin M. Josephy, *The Indian Heritage of America*. New York: Alfred A. Knopf, 1968, p. 334.

Chapter 2: Pushing the Frontier to the Pacific Ocean

29. Quoted in Ron Fisher et al., *Into the Wilderness*. Washington, DC: National Geographic Society, 1978, p. 126.

30. Richard A. Dillon, *Meriwether Lewis: A Biography*. New York: Coward-McCann Inc., 1965, p. xii.

31. Quoted in Erwin R. Blacker, ed., *The Old West in Fact*. New York: Ivan Obolensky, 1962, p. x.

32. Quoted in Fisher et al., *Into the Wilderness*, p. 175.

33. John A. Hawgood, *America's Western Frontiers: The Exploration and Settlement of the Trans-Mississippi West*. New York: Alfred A. Knopf, 1967, p. 94.

34. Quoted in Gary Noy, ed., *Distant Horizon: Documents from the Nineteenth-Century American West*. Lincoln: University of Nebraska Press, 1999, p. 17.

35. Quoted in Dee Brown, *The Westerners*. New York: Holt, Rinehart and Winston, 1974, p. 66.

36. Quoted in Calkins, *The Story of America*, p. 167.

37. Quoted in Kraus, *The United States to 1865*, p. 334.

38. Quoted in Wexler, *Westward Expansion*, p. 101.

39. Quoted in Wexler, *Westward Expansion*, p. 100.

40. Quoted in Heffner, *A Documentary History of the United States*, p. 56.

41. Quoted in Heffner, *A Documentary History of the United States*, p. 56.

42. Wexler, *Westward Expansion*, p. 64.

43. Quoted in Kelley, *The Shaping of the American Past*, p. 153.

44. Quoted in Wexler, *Westward Expansion*, p. 76.

45. Quoted in Davidson et al., *Nation of Nations*, p. 328.

46. Jon E. Lewis, *The Mammoth Book of the West*. New York: Carroll and Graf, 1996, p. xiii.

47. Carter Smith, ed., *The Conquest of the West: A Sourcebook on the American West*. Brookfield, CT: Millbrook Press, 1992, p. 36.

48. Quoted in Heffner, *A Documentary History of the United States*, p. 84.

49. Quoted in Nevins et al., *A Pocket History of the United States*, p. 180.

50. Alan Axelrod, *Chronicle of the Indian Wars: From Colonial Times to Wounded Knee*. New York: Prentice Hall General Reference, 1993, p. 137.

51. Kelley, *The Shaping of the American Past*, p. 156.

52. Quoted in Davidson et al., *Nation of Nations*, p. 394.

Chapter 3: The Lone Star State and the Mormon Migration

53. Quoted in Lewis, *The Mammoth Book of the West*, pp. 68–69.

54. Quoted in Kelley, *The Shaping of the American Past*, p. 9.

55. Quoted in John Hoyt Williams, *Sam Houston: A Biography of the Father of Texas*. New York: Simon and Schuster, 1993, p. 103.

56. Quoted in Henry Steele Commager and Allan Nevins, *The Heritage of America*. Boston: Little, Brown, 1951, p. 590.

57. Quoted in Commager and Nevins, *The Heritage of America*, p. 589.

58. Kelley, *The Shaping of the American Past*, p. 247.

59. Quoted in Harold Faber, *From Sea to Sea: The Growth of the United States*. New York: Charles Scribner's Sons, 1992, p. 91.

60. Williams, *Sam Houston*, p. 143.

61. Quoted in Faber, *From Sea to Sea*, p. 95.

62. Quoted in Faber, *From Sea to Sea*, p. 95.

63. Quoted in Commager and Nevins, *The Heritage of America*, p. 601.

64. Quoted in Williams, *Sam Houston*, p. 155.

65. Quoted in Faber, *From Sea to Sea*, p. 102.

66. Quoted in Kelley, *The Shaping of the American Past*, p. 206.

67. Quoted in Wexler, *Westward Expansion*, p. 158.

68. Quoted in Lewis, *The Mammoth Book of the West*, p. 105.

69. Quoted in Ray Allen Billington, *The Far Western Frontier: 1830–1860*. New York: Harper and Brothers, 1956, p. 199.

70. Quoted in Davidson, *Life in America*, p. 255.

Chapter 4: Manifest Destiny: License to Conquer

71. Quoted in Kelley, *The Shaping of the American Past*, p. 249.

72. Quoted in Davidson et al., *Nation of Nations*, p. 490.

73. Quoted in Davidson et al., *Nation of Nations*, p. 492.

74. Wexler, *Westward Expansion*, p. 120.

75. Quoted in Wexler, *Westward Expansion*, p. 166.

76. Quoted in Lucius Beebe and Charles Clegg, *The American West: The Pictorial Epic of A Continent*. New York: E. P. Dutton, 1955, p. 56.

77. Quoted in Billington, *The Far Western Frontier*, p. 85.

78. Quoted in Faber, *From Sea to Sea*, p. 128.

79. Thomas A. Bailey, *The American Pageant: A History of the Republic*, 5th ed. Lexington, MA: D. C. Heath, 1975, p. 305.

80. Quoted in Smith, *The Conquest of the West*, p. 72.

81. Quoted in Kraus, *The United States to 1865*, p. 445.

82. Quoted in Kelley, *The Shaping of the American Past*, p. 253.

83. Billington, *The Far Western Frontier*, p. 23.

84. Quoted in Bernard De Voto, *The Year of Decision: 1846*. Boston: Little, Brown, 1943, p. 190.

85. Faber, *From Sea to Sea*, p. 131.

86. Kelley, *The Shaping of the American Past*, p. 257.

87. Quoted in Wexler, *Westward Expansion*, p. 165.

88. Quoted in Colbert, *Eyewitness to the American West*, pp. 119–20.

89. Quoted in Commager and Nevins, *The Heritage of America*, p. 603.

90. Hawgood, *America's Western Frontiers*, p. 156.

91. Quoted in Nevins et al., *A Pocket History of the United States*, p. 160.

92. Quoted in Kelley, *The Shaping of the American Past*, p. 279.

Chapter 5: Gold in California Sparks a New Wave of Settlement

93. Quoted in Wexler, *Westward Expansion*, p. 189.

94. Quoted in Bailey, *The American Pageant*, p. 400.

95. Quoted in T. J. Stiles, ed., *In Their Own Words: Warriors and Pioneers*. New York: Berkley Publishing Group, 1996, p. 55.

96. Quoted in Wexler, *Westward Expansion*, p. 139.

97. Quoted in Billington, *The Far Western Frontier*, p. 162.

98. Quoted in Brown, *The Westerners*, p. 120.

99. Quoted in Davidson, *Life in America,* p. 238.

100. Quoted in Lewis, *The Mammoth Book of the West,* p. 112.

101. Quoted in Davidson et al. *Nation of Nations,* p. 511.

102. Quoted in Lewis, *The Mammoth Book of the West,* p. 118.

103. Stiles, *In Their Own Words,* p. 40.

104. Quoted in Hawgood, *America's Western Frontiers,* p. 199.

105. Quoted in Blacker, *The Old West in Fact,* p. 177.

106. Quoted in Faber, *From Sea to Sea,* p. 176.

107. De Voto, *Across the Wide Missouri,* p. 35.

108. Quoted in De Voto, *Across the Wide Missouri,* p. 3.

109. Quoted in Brown, *The Westerners,* p. 102.

110. Davidson et al., *A Nation of Nations,* p. 746.

111. Quoted in Davidson et al., *A Nation of Nations,* p. 748.

112. Quoted in Gerald F. Kreyche, *Visions of the American West.* Lexington: University Press of Kentucky, 1989, p. 217.

113. Quoted in Brown, *The Westerners,* p. 150.

114. Quoted in Brown, *The Westerners,* p. 159.

115. Quoted in Wexler, *Westward Expansion,* p. 228.

Chapter 6: Populating the Plains: Railroads, Cattle, and Farmers

116. Quoted in Hawgood, *America's Western Frontiers,* p. 352.

117. Quoted in Smith, *The Conquest of the West,* p. 86.

118. Quoted in Smith, *The Conquest of the West,* p. 46.

119. Quoted in Hawgood, *America's Western Frontiers,* p. 236.

120. Quoted in Bailey, *The American Pageant,* p. 552.

121. Quoted in Lewis, *The Mammoth Book of the West,* p. 144.

122. Kelley, *The Shaping of the American Past,* p. 398.

123. Davidson et al., *Nation of Nations,* p. 759.

124. Davidson et al., *Nation of Nations,* p. 761.

125. Axelrod, *Chronicle of the Indian Wars,* p. 161.

126. Quoted in Brown, *The Westerners,* p. 197.

127. Quoted in Brown, *The Westerners,* p. 201.

128. Quoted in Wexler, *Westward Expansion,* p. 259.

129. Quoted in Beebe and Clegg, *The American West,* p. 21.

130. Quoted in Hawgood, *America's Western Frontiers,* p. 281.

131. Quoted in Stiles, *In Their Own Words,* p. 158.

132. Quoted in Stiles, *In Their Own Words,* p. 171.

133. Quoted in Lewis, *The Mammoth Book of the West,* p. 423.

134. Quoted in Wexler, *Westward Expansion,* p. 262.

135. Quoted in Davidson et al., *Nation of Nations,* p. 750.

136. Quoted in Stiles, *In Their Own Words,* p. 301.

137. Quoted in Colbert, *Eyewitness to the American West,* p. 199.

Epilogue: The Legacy of the American Frontier

138. Quoted in A. Grove Day, *Hawaii and Its People.* New York: Meredith Press, 1968, p. 216.

139. Quoted in Faber, *From Sea to Sea,* p. 194.

140. Quoted in Martin Ridge, ed., *Frederick Jackson Turner: Wisconsin's Historian of the Frontier.* Madison: State Historical Society of Wisconsin, 1986, p. 26.

141. Quoted in Ridge, *Frederick Jackson Turner,* p. 27.

142. Quoted in Ridge, *Frederick Jackson Turner*, p. 47.

143. Brown, *The Westerners*, p. 214.

144. Davidson et al., *Nation of Nations*, p. 492.

145. Beebe and Clegg, *The American West*, p. 319.

146. Quoted in Wexler, *Westward Expansion*, p. 267.

147. Quoted in Wexler, *Westward Expansion*, p. 135.

148. Brown, *The Westerners*, p. 8.

149. Quoted in Davidson et al., *Nation of Nations*, p. 490.

For Further Reading

Thomas A. Bailey, *The American Pageant: A History of the Republic,* 5th ed. Lexington, MA: D. C. Heath, 1975. A basic history text that is informative and easy to understand.

Lucius Beebe and Charles Clegg, *The American West: The Pictorial Epic of A Continent.* New York: E. P. Dutton, 1955. The story of the West is told in over one thousand illustrations and text. Paintings, editorial cartoons, photographs, and illustrations provide a unique look at the images that helped Americans form their opinions of the old West.

Ray Allen Billington, *The Far Western Frontier: 1830–1860.* New York: Harper and Brothers, 1956. An informative, colorful explanation of Westward Expansion during the period the book covers.

James West Davidson et al., *Nation of Nations: A Narrative History of the American Republic.* 2d ed. New York: McGraw-Hill, 1994. A well-written, interesting history of the United States.

Marshall B. Davidson, *Life in America.* Vol. 1. Boston: Hougton Mifflin, 1951. A well-documented look at not only the history of the nation but the people who settled it.

Harold Faber, *From Sea to Sea: The Growth of the United States.* New York: Charles Scribner's Sons, 1992. The author writes colorfully about Westward Expansion, bringing the people involved in this era alive for the reader.

Thomas Fleming, *Liberty! The American Revolution.* New York: Penguin, 1998. A concise, entertaining telling of the Revolution, with many great pictures and illustrations that help explain this important period in U.S. history.

Eleanor J. Hall, *The Lewis and Clark Expedition.* San Diego, CA: Lucent Books, 1996. A concise, informative narrative of the first full-scale American expedition west of the Mississippi River.

Don Nardo, *Thomas Jefferson.* San Diego, CA: Lucent Books, 1993. An excellent biography; the author uses a wide range of sources to present a balanced portrait of Jefferson.

Carter Smith, ed., *The Conquest of the West: A Sourcebook on the American West.* Brookfield, CT: Millbrook Press, 1992. Explains Westward Expansion one event at a time in a simplified, synopsis-like fashion. Its weakness is that the text is not a continuous narrative to provide transitions between historical happenings.

———, *Exploring the Frontier: A Sourcebook on the American West.* Brookfield, CT: Millbrook Press, 1992. Short articles on the people who first explored the West and some of the things they accomplished.

Works Consulted

Alan Axelrod, *Chronicle of the Indian Wars: From Colonial Times to Wounded Knee.* New York: Prentice Hall General Reference, 1993. A solid historical look at the battles between whites and Native Americans.

Erwin R. Blacker, ed., *The Old West in Fact.* New York: Ivan Obolensky, 1962. A collection of narratives written by people who went westward that allows the reader to understand how individual people felt during this period in history.

Dee Brown, *The Westerners.* New York: Holt, Rinehart and Winston, 1974. A concise look at the opening of the West, including a critical look at some of the issues of Westward Expansion that are controversial today.

Carroll C. Calkins, ed., *The Story of America.* Pleasantville, NY: Reader's Digest, 1975. A comprehensive, interesting examination of the way the nation grew.

David Colbert, ed., *Eyewitness to the American West: From the Aztec Empire to the Digital Frontier in the Words of Those Who Saw It Happen.* New York: Viking, 1998. Excerpts from personal journals, official documents, and other firsthand resource material that help bring the history alive.

Henry Steele Commager and Allan Nevins, *The Heritage of America.* Boston: Little, Brown, 1951. A concise history of the nation by two well-respected historians.

A. Grove Day, *Hawaii and Its People.* New York: Meredith Press, 1968. An informative history of the original Hawaiians who first settled the islands that make up the fiftieth state and the newcomers who arrived in the following centuries.

Bernard De Voto, *Across the Wide Missouri.* Boston: Houghton Mifflin, 1947. Perhaps the finest historical look at the mountain-man era ever written.

———, *The Year of Decision: 1846.* Boston: Little, Brown, 1943. The Pulitzer Prize–winning historian examines the key year in the nation's fulfillment of Manifest Destiny.

Richard A. Dillon, *Meriwether Lewis: A Biography.* New York: Coward-McCann Inc., 1965. A solid biography of the man who helped lead the first cross-country expedition of the United States.

Ron Fisher et al., *Into the Wilderness.* Washington, DC: National Geographic Society, 1978. The author focuses on the explorers and their fact-finding journeys that helped open up the wilderness to settlers.

John A. Hawgood, *America's Western Frontiers: The Exploration and Settlement of the Trans-Mississippi West.* New York: Alfred A. Knopf, 1967. A detailed look at Westward Expansion west of the Mississippi River.

Richard D. Heffner, *A Documentary History of the United States*. Bloomington: Indiana University Press, 1952. A thoughtful, well-documented telling of U.S. history.

Winthrop D. Jordan, Miriam Greenblatt, and John S. Bowes, *The Americans: The History of a People and a Nation*. Evanston, IL: McDouglas, Little, 1985. This book explains U.S. history by focusing on the people who lived it.

Alvin M. Josephy Jr., *The Indian Heritage of America*. New York: Alfred A. Knopf, 1968. A scholarly look at the history of various tribes, including a chapter that sums up how whites conquered and took various portions of the nation.

Robert Kelley, *The Shaping of the American Past: To 1877*. 5th ed. Englewood Cliffs, NJ: Prentice Hall, 1990. The author brings alive U.S. history and makes it easy to understand.

Michael Kraus, *The United States to 1865*. Ann Arbor: University of Michigan Press, 1969. A scholarly telling of U.S. history that explains why events unfolded the way they did.

Gerald F. Kreyche, *Visions of the American West*. Lexington: University Press of Kentucky, 1989. The author explains Westward Expansion by reviewing what motivated its participants.

Jon E. Lewis, *The Mammoth Book of the West*. New York: Carroll and Graf, 1996. A solid, colorful history of Westward Expansion.

Frederick Merk, *History of the Westward Movement*. New York: Alfred A. Knopf, 1978. A detailed, scholarly examination of the nation's growth that delves into the reasons and motivations of those involved.

Samuel Eliot Morison, *The Oxford History of the American People*. New York: Oxford University Press, 1965. A look at U.S. history by one of the nation's most accomplished historians.

Allan Nevins, Henry Steele Commager, with Jeffrey Morris, *A Pocket History of the United States*. 9th ed. New York: Pocket Books, 1992. A condensed history that provides a solid interpretation of the events that shaped America.

Gary Noy, ed., *Distant Horizon: Documents from the Nineteenth-Century American West*. Lincoln: University of Nebraska Press, 1999. This book includes excerpts from speeches, journals, documents, and even fictional works of the period that effectively explain both the facts and the myths of Westward Expansion.

Martin Ridge, ed., *Frederick Jackson Turner: Wisconsin's Historian of the Frontier*. Madison: State Historical Society of Wisconsin, 1986. A biography of this seminal historian that explains the importance of Turner's frontier theory.

T. J. Stiles, ed., *In Their Own Words: Warriors and Pioneers*. New York: Berkley Publishing Group, 1996. A collection of first-person accounts by people involved in Westward Expansion, including Native Americans and U.S. soldiers who fought each other in the West.

Michael V. Uschan, *America's Founders*. San Diego, CA: Lucent Books, 1999. Biographies of Thomas Jefferson and four other people who were responsible for founding the nation and establishing the way it is governed.

————, *The 1910s: A Cultural History of the United States Through the Decades*. San Diego, CA: Lucent Books, 1999. An examination of the history and cultural changes of this important decade in U.S. history.

Sanford Wexler, *Westward Expansion: An Eyewitness History*. New York: Facts On File, 1991. An entertaining but thorough look at how the nation grew, focusing on individuals who made Westward Expansion a reality.

Leonard Wibberley, *Young Man from the Piedmont: The Youth of Thomas Jefferson*. New York: Ariel Books, 1963. Written for young adults, a biography of Thomas Jefferson covering the years 1743–1776.

John Hoyt Williams, *Sam Houston: A Biography of the Father of Texas*. New York: Simon and Schuster, 1993. A fine biography of the historical figure who was chiefly responsible for the birth of Texas.

Index

Picture Credits

About the Author

Michael V. Uschan has written eleven books. His previous works for Lucent include *America's Founders* and *The Importance of John F. Kennedy*. Mr. Uschan began his career as a writer and editor with United Press International, a wire service that provided stories to newspapers, radio, and television. Because journalism is sometimes called "history in a hurry," he considers writing history books a natural extension of the skills he has developed through his many years as a working journalist. He and his wife, Barbara, live in Franklin, Wisconsin, a suburb of Milwaukee.